"I was enthusiastic about the first edition *An Army of Ordinary People* but this second edition is even better. Like the first edition, it is extremely practical and inspiring. This edition is even more incisive and relevant with regard to some of the most distinctive and essential characteristics of living out one's spiritual life in a simple expression of church. The style and content match the message. Even more important, the author's life reflects the truth of this book. I heartily recommend you read this and give copies to your friends."

CURTIS SERGEANT *vice president of e3 International, e3 Partners Ministry*

"A man or woman with a God story is not the prisoner of someone else's theory of church. The power of the stories told in this book is that they are true, they are happening now, and they are taking place all over the world. God is up to something and I don't want to miss it!"

FLOYD MCCLUNG *founder of All Nations Family*

"In *An Army of Ordinary People*, Felicity Dale reminds us that God uses common, everyday people to extend His Kingdom. Writing in the language of the common person, she relates with every one of us who desire to have a meaningful walk with God. She shares real stories of regular folks whom God is using to infect their communities with the love, care, and compassion of Christ. This book will allow everyone to relate with 'life in Christ.' It's simple; anyone can do it!"

MICHAEL STEELE *cofounder of The Ploion Group*

"Tony and Felicity Dale are the real deal. When they speak, I listen. What they are teaching, the church as a whole must get. I am obsessed with the Kingdom and so are they. They move far beyond structural issues to core issues of how the body of Christ operates. Every church must be a 'simple church,' regardless of structure. There is so much that they bring to the whole body. My biggest fear is that pastors who have buildings—like myself—will not hear what the Dales are saying because the form is different. Forget the form. Study the function and implement it in your context—and watch God move in powerful ways!"

BOB ROBERTS *senior pastor of Northwood Church, Keller, Texas*

"The age of the ordained has passed; welcome to the day of the ordinary. God delights in using ordinary people to do extraordinary things because it reveals His own power and glory. This book reveals how God is already on the move in North America. My hope is that you will be so enthused after reading this book that you will go out and do something worthy of placement in the next volume!"

NEIL COLE *founder of Church Multiplication Associates and executive director of CMAResources.org; author of* Organic Church *and* Church 3.0

"In this book, Felicity Dale has conveyed the Spirit of both the original and the future church. In the personal stories of people who trusted God's leadership we can catch a glimpse of how God will revive His church N. J tion, no matter how broad the ministry offerir the multiplication of groups that put worship ordinary Christians in the midst of daily life."

JOEL HUNTER *senior pastor of Northland Chu*

"This book is a forecast of what church will look like for many in the emerging generation: a missional church without walls where every Christ follower is disciple in the Great Commandment and empowered in the Great Commission. Put these stories in the hands of young people and watch them make history for God!"

JAESON MA *CSO of Asian Digital Ventures Network*

"I am telling you up front: Felicity Dale is dangerous. Behind the veneer of this soft-spoken, former medical doctor from the UK, you will encounter a bold captain in God's army telling the fascinating story of God completely revamping His church. In this book, it's not the superstars looking down at 'poor you' selling you some other magic red button to press to make your life into what it should be. Instead, it's the ordinary men and women already enlisted in God's breathtaking Kingdom endeavor, smiling, hooting, and waving at you across your very own fence, inviting you, too, to come and change the world with them. So don't buy this book, sit back and relax, as this kind of stuff could turn you upside down. Which is—be honest!—exactly what you need."

WOLFGANG SIMSON *author of* The House Church Book *and* The Starfish Manifesto

"It's always been God's strategy to use ordinary people to change the world, mainly because he doesn't have anything else to choose from. This inspiring, practical, and accessible book not only tells the stories of world-changers, but invites us to count ourselves in too."

JEFF LUCAS *author, speaker, broadcaster*

"Stories give hope. Stories give courage. And *An Army of Ordinary People* is a book full of stories that do both. To know that there are men and women, just like you and me, engaged in God's mission to redeem and renew their neighborhoods, workplaces, hangouts, and cities, is encouraging and invigorating! I would recommend this book to anyone who wants a glimpse into what it means to be an ordinary radical shaped by the mission of God, starting and multiplying missional communities that can transform every square inch of our society."

MICHAEL STEWART *pastor of missional communities at The Austin Stone Community Church, Austin, Texas*

"It is no stretch to say that this book grabbed me by the shirt, shook me up, and set me down facing a new direction. Let me be clear: I don't mean to say that I experienced a 'paradigm shift.' Far, far better than that, a half dozen loosely related passions and hunches fell into place that afternoon. I spent the better part of the next two days alternating between brooding over what I had read and trumpeting its values to everyone in talking distance."

RALPH MOORE *pastor of Hope Chapel Kaneohe Bay, Hawaii, and author of* How to Multiply Your Church

"*An Army of Ordinary People* is a contemporary book of Acts. As I read it, I was drawn again to the compelling nature of the church as simple, relational, reproducible, powerful—what we yearn for."

CAROL DAVIS *director of Lifeline Initiatives*

an army of
ORDINARY PEOPLE

Stories of Real-Life Men and Women
Simply Being the Church

FELICITY DALE

BARNA

AN IMPRINT OF TYNDALE HOUSE PUBLISHERS, INC.

Visit Tyndale's exciting Web site at www.tyndale.com.

TYNDALE is a registered trademark of Tyndale House Publishers, Inc.

Barna and the Barna logo are trademarks of George Barna.

BarnaBooks is an imprint of Tyndale House Publishers, Inc.

An Army of Ordinary People: Stories of Real-Life Men and Women Simply Being the Church

Designed by Jessie McGrath

Edited by Bonne Steffen

Published in association with the literary agency of Fedd and Company Inc., 9759 Concord Pass, Brentwood, TN 37027.

To protect the privacy of those who have shared their stories with the author, some names have been changed. Still, every story in this book is true.

Library of Congress Cataloging-in-Publication Data

Dale, Felicity.
    An army of ordinary people : stories of real-life men and women simply being the church / Felicity Dale.
        p. cm.
    Includes bibliographical references.
    ISBN 978-1-4143-2279-7 (sc)
    1. Non-institutional churches. 2. Christian leadership. I. Title.
    BV601.9.D36 2010
    262′.26—dc22   2009054159

Printed in the United States of America

16 15 14 13 12 11 10
 7   6   5   4   3   2   1

This book is dedicated to all those who work in the trenches, many of whom have stories like the ones in this book. In particular it is dedicated to the memory of Lillie Villarreal, a true person of peace with a heart as big as Texas, who made us part of her family.

Contents

Foreword

ASK ANY GREAT teacher or coach the most effective way to help people learn, and you'll get a uniform answer: through stories. Stories motivate, captivate, and educate. A good narrative grabs our imagination, helps us to relate to the characters, and improves our recall of the principles. As the possessor of perfect knowledge and understanding, perhaps that was why Jesus Christ relied so heavily upon stories as His primary instructional method.

An Army of Ordinary People is a book of stories that will help you grasp why organic churches are growing in popularity and increasing in influence. Millions of Americans want to know how to *be* the church rather than simply *go* to church. This is a book that takes you by the hand and shows how. With a cast of characters as varied as those to whom Jesus ministered, *Army* innocently highlights the fact that the "simple church" approach is viable for anyone who is serious about knowing God more deeply.

Our research indicates that relatively few people—certainly less than one out of every five, depending upon how tightly you define it—are gifted as leaders. That has been one of the limitations raised about the possible spread of simple churches; there are not enough genuine leaders to initiate and develop simple churches. But Felicity Dale's stories about the simple churches that she and her husband, Tony, have known are proof that organic ministries operate differently than anything we have seen on this continent in our lifetime.

The ability to assemble people and direct their efforts within these nontraditional ministries is less dependent upon organizational competencies such as public speaking, management prowess, and fund-raising than upon such spiritual commitments as availability, faithfulness, and obedience. If you search for a common thread among those who lead these churches, you'll find that it is their determination to love and serve God and His people. These people are revolutionaries. They are a spiritual remnant that does not care about the prevailing practices and customs of the church world as much as they care about the presence of the Holy Spirit, the directives in God's Word, and participating in a community of people whose hearts yearn for God and will not be satisfied until they connect with Him.

These are simply ordinary people doing ordinary stuff that is enabling God to produce an extraordinary result. Do you want to be one of them?

The people described by Felicity in these pages are what is often referred to as "early adopters"—they are among the first people in our midst who have embraced a new approach to following Jesus on American soil. But they are far from being the totality of the movement. Our national studies not only show that house churches and other forms of organic faith are growing rapidly, but that tens of millions of Americans are similarly open to new types of faith experiences and expressions.

For instance, half of all adults (50 percent) contend that "a growing number of people I know are tired of the usual type of church experience." In fact, the numbers of Americans who are doing something about it—or are considering taking some type of responsive action—are unprecedented. The percentage of adults involved in a house church has more than doubled in the past decade. Two out of every three adults (64 percent) say they are "completely open to carrying out and pursuing their faith in an environment or structure that differs from that of a typical church." And an overwhelming three out of four adults (75 percent) say they sense that "God is motivating people to stay connected with Him, but in different ways and through different types of experiences than in the past."

The organic church movement is not religious activity run by professionals, based on programs and dependent upon big budgets to maintain buildings and facilities. It is, as the name "simple church" implies, an uncomplicated gathering of like-hearted people who want to follow Christ and worship together, growing in their faith and relationships. Instead of becoming predictable, bureaucratic, or even well organized, simple churches strive to be authentic and to be driven forward by the Spirit of God.

To experience what God has in store for them, those in the organic church movement employ the simplest but most profound of concepts: waiting on God's Spirit, following His will, serving people, worshiping without fanfare or self-consciousness, enjoying intimate relationships with other Christ followers, and making faith a lifestyle rather than an event. They believe that what the Bible says is true, and because they have the eyes of faith, they perceive and receive miracles from God. In fact, their smaller context for ministry allows them to test their faith more intensely and to observe and revel in the amazing outcomes in ways that are often impossible in a larger setting.

Organic churches are not perfect. They have issues, like any gathering of people or any group that seeks to accomplish something significant. But one of the beautiful realizations that *Army* brings to light is that simple churches are not seeking to redefine "the church" as much as they are engaged in returning it to its original, biblical form—sometimes unknowingly. The stories and commentary you'll read in this book will help you to understand why the early church was more similar to the simple church model than to the programmatic church that is so common today. Perhaps both have value in today's marketplace. The simple church certainly has as much claim to the title "church" as does the more conventional form.

Take some time to read about Hank, the produce manager; Tony and Kathy, the tenderhearted doctor and nurse; Elizabeth and Scott, the good neighbors; Jordan, the college student; Josh, the wayward gang member; David, the maintenance supervisor; Jim, the church elder—and many more. These are people like you and me—not "professional Christians" whose training has prepared them to plant churches and build infrastructures, but common citizens whose hearts yearn for the presence and guidance of God.

I'm willing to bet that you will read many of these stories and think to yourself, *I could do that.* You'll read the experiences outlined in these pages and be astounded by what God has done. If you're like me, some of the testimonies will bring tears to your eyes. This is a book that merely describes some of the incredible, life-transforming work that God is doing in our midst today. He looks for people who are looking for Him, and blesses those who want to be a blessing to others. It's not, as they say, rocket science. All it takes is some faith and a little bit of courage.

If you want to be part of this movement of God, do exactly what these practitioners have done: trust God enough to let Him direct your journey. The journeys depicted by Felicity show that it takes no special coaching or reservoir of Bible knowledge. It takes a willing heart, an open mind, and a bit of determination. As Felicity shows us, the lives of those who allow God to lead them will, thankfully, never be the same again.

George Barna

Preface

WRITING THIS BOOK has been both a privilege and a humbling experience for me. When I first began thinking about writing a book of stories that would illustrate house or simple church principles, I had no idea where the journey would take me. I spent many hours talking with the people whose lives are portrayed here, and was often profoundly moved and challenged by what I heard.

Some of the names in the stories have been changed, for reasons that will become obvious.

This book is not aimed at theologians or people who want to read deep and complicated philosophical or theological discussions. There are many great books about simple church written from those viewpoints. Instead, this book is written for ordinary people, like the ones whose stories are told here. My hope is that anyone reading this book will gain a vision to join the ranks of this army of people with outrageous faith who have dared to take God at His word, make disciples, and join Him in building His church.

This book is not for the religious or fainthearted. It will offend those who prefer not to cross paths with people who are not like themselves. This book is for believers who are in the trenches, willing to get their hands dirty in the pain and glory of life. It is for those who are not afraid to go where Jesus did—people who are willing to let God be God and to do things His way.

My thanks go to all those who were willing to risk opening their lives to share their stories.

This book belongs to them.

Felicity Dale

Introduction

THIS IS A book of stories. Stories are compelling; they grab you. Jesus used stories to illustrate spiritual principles again and again. He told stories people could relate to—stories about things His hearers would be familiar with—crops and sheep, yeast and coins. When we tell stories, people remember them, even if they forget everything else we say.

Each of the stories in this book is about the life of an ordinary person God has used to make disciples and gather them into a simple church. The stories are a snapshot in time, a brief glimpse at a relevant part of that person's journey. You will notice that very few of the people are in so-called "full-time ministry." Most of them are like you and me—they get up in the morning and go to work all day. They raise families. They have their share of problems and frustrations. They are not spiritual superstars.

But something happens when they decide to reach out to unbelievers to make disciples and start a church. All of a sudden, their stories shift into the extraordinary! God accepts their offers to yield their lives to Him. He then turns their lives—and their world—upside down.

Across the world, God is speaking the same message to people.

He no longer wants it to be church as usual. He wants His church back! Everywhere, people are catching a vision of a church that is simpler, that meets around the dining table in a home, during lunchtime in an office, or over a hot beverage in a coffeehouse. It is a vibrant community, based on building relationships and following the leading of the Holy Spirit. Are all of these simple expressions of His body healthy? Do all of them survive? Not every one. They are often messy and seemingly insignificant, but together they represent something that God is doing worldwide.

An army of anonymous people—nameless and faceless—is rising up. They are willing to take God at His word and are attempting to reach their world with the good news that Jesus still opens blind eyes and sets captives free. Under the command of their Captain, they are following Him wherever He leads. He is taking them into unexplored territory where not-yet-believers are waiting to hear about the Lifegiver and have their lives transformed by Him. Jesus is challenging them to gather this "new wine" into the new wineskins of small, caring communities of His people that He calls church. He promises that His presence will be there with them.

Each story illustrates a principle (or two) about how to make disciples that gather as a simple church. My hope and prayer in writing this book is that anyone reading it can identify with one of the stories and say, "I can do that!"

1

GOD USES ORDINARY PEOPLE TO DO THE EXTRAORDINARY

The Produce Manager Who Planted Churches

For they could see that they were ordinary men with no special training in the Scriptures. They also recognized them as men who had been with Jesus. — ACTS 4:13

These who have turned the world upside down have come here too. — ACTS 17:6, NKJV

☼ In any land, when laborers, mechanics, clerks, or truck drivers teach the Bible, lead in prayer, tell what God has done for them, or exhort the brethren, the Christian religion looks and sounds natural to ordinary men. Whatever unpaid laymen, earning their living as others do, subject to the same hazards and bound by the same work schedules, lack in correctness of Bible teaching or beauty of prayers, they more than make up for by their intimate contact with their own people.

— DONALD MCGAVRAN, *Understanding Church Growth*

IF YOU HAD met Hank in the large grocery store where he worked, you would have found a soft-spoken, unassuming man. In fact, the produce manager was so introverted, his friends jokingly said that it was a real achievement if they could get him to string three words together.

Years before, Hank had played in the worship band at a legacy[1] church, but eventually drifted away. When a friend learned that Hank wasn't attending church, he invited Hank to visit his church that met in a home. To Hank's surprise, an old friend was leading the group—Hank and Doug had been in the worship band together. Now Doug pastored a legacy church and also led the home-based group.

"A couple of us guys get together at Starbucks every week," Doug told Hank. "We read some chapters out of the Bible during the week. Then on Fridays we get together to hold each other accountable for what is going on in our lives and to pray for our friends. We call it a life transformation group. Would you like to join us?"

As Hank devoured Scripture, prayed for non-Christian friends, and confessed his struggles to his accountability partners each week, things started happening.

The first change was unexpected and devastating. Hank's wife of more than twenty years left and then divorced him. Drawing on God's strength, Hank threw himself even more vigorously into what the Lord was doing in his life, and his spiritual life accelerated like wildfire.

"I'm not sure what's going on," Hank admitted to Doug one day. "For no reason that I can figure out, other employees at work keep asking me to pray for them. They never used to do that. There are other Christians around who are much more vocal about their faith than I am, but I'm the one people confide in. What do you think is going on?"

"Do you remember what we learned in our *Experiencing God*[2] Bible study?" Doug asked. "We need to see what God is doing and join Him in it. I think God is doing this. I wonder what He has in mind. Do you think some of your friends from work would be willing to get together with you to study the Bible?"

Hank wasn't a trained pastor. He had never gone to college, let alone seminary. After graduating from high school, he had joined the military. Hank knew he still had so much to learn about God. Could he really start a church?

When Hank asked the coworkers for whom he had been praying if they wanted to meet with him in his home, only one of them said yes. But when Hank mentioned the idea to several of his family members, they wanted to come and bring some of their friends. So Hank started his first church, with a majority of people who did not know Jesus. One by one, they gave their hearts to the Lord and then began experiencing remarkable transformations in their lives.

> We need to see what God is doing and join Him in it.

Two months after the church began, Hank was carrying a large, heavy pallet at work. Not seeing a hose that was lying on the ground, he tripped and fell, shattering his ankle. For the next three months, he was confined to his bed. Hank used the time to pray and read his Bible as well as other Christian books. The church continued to meet, with members gathering around Hank in his small apartment.

One day Hank's mother came by to check on him. During the visit she asked, "Would you start a church in my house too?" She lived about twenty miles away. Hank's second church was a real family affair—many of his fifteen siblings and their children joined. A month later, some of Hank's grown children who had never been involved in church asked if he would do something similar for them.

But God wasn't done yet. Three months later, a woman telephoned Hank. "I met your son the other day, and he was telling me about how you run churches in people's homes," she said. "I would love to have something like that in my home. Would you be willing to show me how?" A fourth church was born, grew rapidly, and spawned two other groups. In less than a year Hank, the guy people teased because he never said anything, had birthed six churches!

Witnessing God's Healing

Hank and two other Christians were at the hospital one day to visit José, a friend who was in a coma from a drug overdose—a botched suicide attempt. (The twenty-one-year-old had been heavily involved in gangs and drugs most of his life.) When they arrived at the ICU, a group of doctors was gathered around José's bed, preparing permission forms to harvest his organs. José was brain-dead; the doctors had just pulled the plug on his life-support machines. The grieving relatives were waiting in the hallway.

"Why don't we pray for José anyway?" one of Hank's friends suggested. The small group of believers gathered around the bed, laid their hands on José, and prayed, "Lord, when You walked this earth, You healed the sick and raised the dead! Will You come and show Your power again in this situation?" Then Hank and his friends left to get something to eat.

When they returned to the ICU, there was a lot of activity and an air of suppressed excitement. One of José's relatives came up to Hank and his friends with tears streaming down his cheeks.

"You will not believe what just happened! Shortly after you left, José opened his eyes. The doctors couldn't believe it. All their tests indicated he was dead. Look at him now!"

Hank couldn't believe what he saw. José was sitting up in bed eating a Popsicle.

On another occasion, Hank prayed for a girl with a serious brain tumor and she was healed. Hank had grown into a man of faith who knew beyond any shadow of doubt that God heals the sick and raises the dead.

But there is something else you need to know about Hank. A few years ago, Hank was diagnosed with Lou Gehrig's disease, a debilitating condition characterized by progressive loss of muscle control. For some time, Hank had been having difficulty performing simple physical tasks. He never fully recovered from his broken ankle and had an increasingly tough time walking. Yet most of the churches Hank started were planted during the years when his physical condition was steadily deteriorating.

Eventually he needed a wheelchair, was unable to drive, and required personal assistance for several hours each day.

> Hank had grown into a man of faith who knew that God heals.

During this time, Hank developed other leaders who were able to take responsibility for the churches. Members of the network helped to take care of him, and the churches frequently met in his apartment around his wheelchair. Hank remained unfailingly cheerful and excited about what the Lord was doing in his life and the lives of people God had touched through him.

Although Hank died in December 2007, his story lives on.

Ordinary People; Extraordinary Results

All over the world, God is using ordinary believers like Hank—or you and me—to plant churches. In countries such as China[3] and India,[4] among others, hundreds of thousands of people become Christians every year because of the multiplication of these simpler forms of church.

It is no longer exclusively up to the trained professional who has been to Bible college or seminary to advance the Kingdom. Housewives and factory workers, businesspeople and doctors are leaving their comfortable pews and heading into their worlds to make disciples. Many non-Christians who would never darken the door of a church building have no problem meeting in small groups called simple, organic, or house churches.

Just imagine what would happen if ordinary men and women by the thousands were equipped to replicate that growth in home after home.

About one-third of Christians in the United States are not attending an organized church, but they have not given up on their Lord. Imagine what could happen if this group caught hold of the simple church vision and discipled not-yet-believers in their own homes within their circle of friends.

> *God will use anyone who is willing to advance His Kingdom.*

There are many people within legacy churches who have a passion to reach out to those who do not know Jesus. Imagine what could happen if they were trained and released to start these simpler forms of church.

God will use anyone who is willing to advance His Kingdom. The question is, are we ready to let God use us?

When I look at Hank's life, I know I have no excuse!

2

WHAT IS CHURCH?

The Couple Who Learned from Their Mistakes

For where two or three gather together as my followers, I am there among them. — MATTHEW 18:20

✹ When two or three born-again believers come together in His name, Jesus is *in the midst*. Jesus in the midst is CHURCH! It is a different experience than Jesus within. We cannot experience Jesus in the midst while we are alone. We can only experience Jesus in the midst when we are in company with others; at least one or two others who are called by His name.

But is it a church in the fullest sense of the word? Yes, it is a church in the fullest sense of the word. It is the basic church. You can have more than two or three and it is still a church, . . . but it does not become more of a church because there are more than two or three people in the congregation. It only becomes a bigger church.

— ROBERT FITTS, *The Church in the House*

"HAS THE LORD said anything to you on this trip?" My husband, Tony, and I were 35,000 feet above the Atlantic Ocean, flying back home to England from California, where we had been speaking at various churches.

"Yes," I replied. "I sensed Him speaking to me about our future. How about you?"

"I sensed the same thing," he said. "You go first."

"I think the Lord is telling us to move to the States!"

"That's what He told me, too!"

This was not the first time the Lord had spoken to us in this way.

"I've been thinking about CiCP," Tony continued. "Derek is the one person who could lead it. Maybe the Lord wants us to hand over leadership in the UK to him. Then we could move to the States to start it there."

"Derek's such a busy doctor," I commented. "How would he possibly have time to take on those extra responsibilities?"

Christians in the Caring Professions (CiCP) was a ministry Tony had led for many years in England. Its purpose was to help doctors, nurses, and others in the medical field bring their faith into their professional lives. Participants were taught how to lead their patients to the Lord or how to pray with them for healing—all within the context of the doctor's office. Over the years, God greatly blessed this ministry. Thousands of doctors and others with similar callings attended the conferences that we ran each year in England and in several other countries. Tony was working full-time for CiCP when we sensed the Lord's direction to leave England.

We had been home for less than twenty-four hours when Tony received a phone call from Derek. "I was in church yesterday morning," he said, "and someone gave me a word from the Lord that I have a major change coming in my life. The more I've thought and prayed over it, the more I sensed I should contact you. Do you have any idea what this might mean?" Both Tony and Derek were amazed at the Lord's clear leading.

Five months later, Tony and I, our four young children, and twelve of the biggest boxes the airline would allow arrived in Austin, Texas. We didn't know anyone in Texas, let alone Austin. Most of our American friends lived on the East Coast, so it didn't make a lot of sense to us. Still, we both knew this was where the Lord wanted us to be.

It was a good thing the Lord led us as clearly as He did, because after dumping us in Texas, He returned to England! And He did not show up in our lives again for nine long and painful years.

It wasn't that we didn't like living in the States—we loved it! We loved the people, the country, and the food. What we couldn't handle was that God was missing from our lives. Although we didn't realize it at the time, we had been involved in a revival in England—a church-planting movement. Beginning in the late sixties, churches emerged spontaneously at a grassroots level throughout the UK. They started in homes, spawning the name "the British house church movement." As the churches grew, the groups moved into buildings. All of the groups were characterized by deep fellowship, by "nonreligious Christianity" (Christianity not based on rules and regulations, but motivated by the life of the Spirit within), and by team leadership. In the churches we were involved in, one of the key concepts practiced was the priesthood of all believers—everyone participates in the gathering.

During this time of revival, Tony and I helped to start a church at Barts Hospital, where we both were students training to be physicians. Tony left Barts for two years to go to Bible school (later returning to finish his medical training), so I graduated first. I began practicing in the East End of London, a poverty-stricken part of the city. There we worked with other believers to plant another church. The numbers grew in that church because patients found the Lord. Like most of the other house churches across the UK, it quickly became one of the largest churches in the area.

> All of the UK house churches were characterized by deep fellowship, nonreligious Christianity, and team leadership.

The Holy Spirit worked through the members of CiCP; thousands of doctors and their patients were touched by the Spirit's power. For example, many Christian doctors became involved with us in our area of London, which at that time was a very socially deprived community of around 150,000 people. One day we did the math and calculated that any person getting sick in our area stood a one-in-three chance of sitting down with a Christian doctor looking for an opportunity to talk to his patients about Jesus.

When our family landed in the States, we had moved from a place of outstanding blessing and influence into a spiritual desert. The first nine years we participated in several good legacy churches, but we just did not fit in. The Christianity we had known was so different, and we made so many mistakes. It was as though the Lord gave us a crash course in American church life. He also took the opportunity to deal with our characters!

Not only did we fail to integrate into the church, but everything we thought God wanted to accomplish through us in the States resulted in nothing. CiCP went over like a lead balloon—only the Holy Spirit could have shut the doors as firmly as He did. And no one wanted to hire an unlicensed physician. (It would have taken us four to five years of additional training to get our U.S. medical licenses.)

I would like to tell you that I handled this situation with grace and dignity, but I didn't. To start with, I repented of everything—real or imaginary—that I could think of. Then I begged the Lord to show us where we were sinning. Finally, I whined and complained about our lack of finances. I wept over the loss of the relationships we had known back in England. I shouted angrily at the Lord. Nothing. The heavens remained silent for a long, long time.

> We gave the Lord a deadline. Either things changed or it was back to England.

We finally arrived at the point where we gave the Lord a deadline (not a course we recommend to anyone). Either things changed or we were on our way back to England. At least there we could earn a decent living!

It's Okay to Start a Church

But then, things started to change. Most important of all, God started communicating with us again.

"You will have the privilege of being part of a move of My Spirit again," was one of the first things He told us.

Was God about to do something amazing in North America?

When we had moved to the States, we had started a business to generate income. It was moderately successful, and we had a considerable number of business associates, many of whom were unbelievers. In fact, for the first time in many years, the majority of our friends did not know the Lord. Now Tony proposed pulling a group of our business leaders together to see if we could introduce some spiritual concepts into the mix.

"Come over Friday evening for pizza. We're going to look at business principles and how to handle wealth. For our discussions we'll be using a book written by a man who is supposed to be the wisest person who ever lived," he told them.

So every Friday evening for a year a dozen of us met, ate pizza, and had a lively discussion on the book of Proverbs. There was only one rule: there were no rules. Everyone's opinion mattered. There were no wrong answers. But if the Bible had anything to say about whatever we were discussing, then it would be our authority on that subject.

The discussions were invigorating and wide-ranging. It

didn't take long before the Bible was accepted as the final word on any topic. The seed of the Kingdom truly is the Word of God,[1] and soon that seed started to bear fruit.

I recall one memorable evening when two members of the group, both ex–drug dealers, were intensely discussing why some of their drug deals hadn't worked. "We weren't following the principles in Proverbs!" they concluded. Tony and I struggled not to laugh out loud.

> The Bible was our authority on whatever we were discussing.

Over the course of that year, each person in the group surrendered his or her life to Jesus!

At that time, we were attending a legacy church that met in a hotel about thirty minutes away from our home. They were doing a great job of incorporating our new believers into what was going on there. But when they physically moved to a building twenty minutes farther away, we decided we had to do something different. We sat down with Trey, the senior pastor, and shared our concerns.

"Why don't you start your own church?" he suggested. "You've done it before in England. The best means of evangelism is to start a church."[2]

Was this the right course to take? Should we gather these new disciples together at our home rather than traveling to the other side of town?

At the time we had four teenagers, with the two youngest living at home. What would we do about them?

We decided to start a "Breakfast Bible Club." Our kids

invited all their friends from our neighborhood, promising them a delicious home-cooked breakfast.

We decided to meet on Sunday morning. We wanted to reach the non-Christian kids, and we figured that the kids from Christian families would be in church on Sunday mornings. Soon our house was full every Sunday morning. The kids' parents were delighted because they could sleep in. The kids came for the food, but they stayed for the activities, all based on the Bible. It wasn't long before some of the kids became Christians; the number grew to fifteen or more. Some of them brought their parents or other family members—they had noticed that their kids' lives were changing and wanted to know why.

Growing Pains

Eventually we merged the Friday night group of businesspeople and the Sunday morning kids' group and wound up with fifty-plus people in our living room, hallway, kitchen and dining area, and up the stairs—occupying every conceivable space. We ate together, spent time in worship and sharing, and then divided into small groups to study the Bible. One of the families from across the street became involved, and they opened up their home so that we could divide into multiple smaller groups whenever needed. We prayed for one another and God answered. Occasionally, we would see miracles happen.

One Sunday morning, God impressed on someone[3] in the group that one of the people in the house was about to experience a life-threatening condition. We were all concerned; someone prayed specifically over John, one of the men in the church.

During the course of that week, John started to bleed from one of his eyes. When he went to the doctor for tests, a tumor was discovered behind his eyeball.

The following Sunday, several people in the church prayed for John to be healed. He was scheduled for a biopsy at the hospital the next day. When doctors repeated the tests to find the exact location of the tumor for the biopsy, the tumor was gone. God had healed John!

Our times of meeting together were never boring. They were based on 1 Corinthians 14:26: "When you meet together, one will sing, another will teach, another will tell some special revelation God has given, one will speak in tongues, and another will interpret what is said. But everything that is done must strengthen all of you." Everyone took part, including the kids. The Holy Spirit would often speak most clearly through them.

One day I asked Tony, "What are we going to do? We've outgrown our house."

During our nine years of wandering in the "wilderness," we often talked about how meaningful the early days of our church planting in England had been, when the churches we started were still small. It seemed so much easier to obey the New Testament in a small-group context. How could you bear one another's burdens[4] or teach and counsel one another[5] if there were a hundred or, for that matter, even fifty of you? Not only that, we knew that in countries such as China, the church was expanding very rapidly through the multiplication of small churches.

> How could you bear one another's burdens if there were a hundred of you?

"Well, we could rent a building and get larger," Tony said. "Or we could try to multiply smaller churches that meet in homes or wherever people spend most of their lives."

"What is a church anyway?" I asked. "Suppose a church really is how it is described in Matthew 18—that when two or three are gathered together in His name, Jesus is there in the midst of them. If that is real church, then anyone can start one."

"That would make more sense of the New Testament passages that explain how you should behave toward one another," Tony added. "You really can only do that in the context of a small group."

This paradigm shift in our thinking seemed to be what the Scriptures instructed.

So we made the first of many mistakes in our experience with simple churches. We split the group down the middle. For about a year, people came to us complaining that it felt like they had been through a divorce. Relationships were so deep and meaningful within the group that we really were like family. (Today we prefer to birth a daughter church once a person of peace—such as Rosa in chapter 6—is found who can help create a church in their home.)

Over the next year, we only grew three churches. At this rate, it would take us forever to make an impact on our community!

Learning from Other Nations

In February 2000, we were watching a news report about the devastating floods in Mozambique, a country in the southern part of Africa. Half of the country was under water.

"That's where Rolland and Heidi Baker are!" Tony exclaimed. "I wonder if there's anything I can do to help." Rolland and Tony had grown up together on the mission field and attended the same boarding school for missionary kids in Taiwan. By this stage, the Lord had given Tony and me the idea for a business that had become successful enough for us to be able to leave for extended periods of time.

We immediately began collecting money for medicine and were able to purchase tens of thousands of dollars' worth of pharmaceuticals for pennies on the dollar. Less than two weeks later, Tony and Kathy, a friend of ours who is a nurse, flew to Mozambique.

Even without devastating floods, the people of Mozambique are desperately poor. Most families live in small huts made from reeds, with mud floors. They have no furniture, no electricity or running water, and most of them do not even own a change of clothing.

Rolland and Heidi had been asked to oversee some of the refugee camps set up for people displaced by the floods.

Whenever they went to one of the camps, they preached the gospel, and God moved powerfully. Hundreds, and then thousands, of people in the camps gave their lives to the Lord.

Tony and Kathy worked out of the orphanage that Rolland and Heidi had built in Maputu, the capital city. But every day, the United Nations flew Tony and Kathy by helicopter to a different refugee camp located on higher ground. They often were the first medical people to arrive, bringing supplies of food, blankets, and Bibles. Sometimes there was a mini-stampede for the items. The people were often more interested in the Bibles than in the food!

Tony and Kathy set up clinics under trees or in old army tents or buildings when they were available. People seemed to appear from nowhere out of the bush. Several times during the day, Tony and Kathy stopped their medical work and preached the gospel through an interpreter.

"Some of you are sick because germs you cannot see are affecting your bodies," Tony told the group. "Even though you cannot see sin, it's like the germs that are making you sick. Sin is choosing to live life your own way rather than the way God, your Creator, wants you to live. That sin causes spiritual death in your life. But God loves you so much that He sent His Son, Jesus, to die for you on a cross; He took this death for you. If you will surrender your life to Him, He will take away your sin and you can have a new life. If any of you would like to give your life to Him, raise your hand."

Everyone raised their hands.

"No, no! You don't understand. This means giving up your witch doctors and your other gods. You need to give your life totally to Jesus. Who still wants to give their lives to Him?"

Again, everyone raised their hands. Tony prayed for them, and the people rejoiced as only they can in Africa—with singing and dancing. By the time Tony and Kathy left, there might be a hundred or more new believers. (Later, Rolland and Heidi sent pastors who had been trained at the orphanage to assist the new churches.[6] Today, there are 10,000 churches in Mozambique that can trace their roots back to the work Rolland and Heidi began there.)

Tony e-mailed me nearly every day to report what was happening. His firsthand accounts were widely distributed; our local newspaper did a two-page spread on the devastation and needs in Mozambique. Our small network of simple churches sponsored a clothes collection for the refugees. Soon we were receiving bundles of used clothes from various legacy churches and schools around the city. We eventually sent a forty-foot container crammed full of clothing to be distributed.

It was a life-changing experience to be in the center of the revival in Mozambique—not only for Tony and Kathy on their trip in March, but also for me and two of our children when we returned with Tony in June. Rolland and Heidi have continued to see God at work both in Mozambique and in neighboring countries like Malawi and Tanzania.[7]

Amazing miracles and healings are occurring: the blind see, the deaf hear, and even the dead have been raised to life! In Mozambique, church didn't happen in a building or in a house. Most often it was church under a tree! But it was real church nonetheless.

In October of that same year, Tony and I were invited to India by a church planter named Shalem who had come across our names on the Internet. We felt led to go.

India is an amazing country with people everywhere! The traffic alone has to be experienced to be believed. We concluded that there is only one rule on the roads: the larger vehicle wins—unless, of course, there is a cow involved. Every driver keeps his hand jammed on the horn, so the noise is almost deafening. And talk about maximizing transportation! It was the first time in our lives that we saw six people riding on one motorized scooter.

> In Mozambique, church didn't happen in a house. Usually it was church under a tree!

It was also Tony's and my first encounter with severe urban poverty. Back then, Chennai (formerly Madras), the city we flew into, had a population of ten million. One million people lived on the streets (literally sleeping on the sidewalk), and four million more lived in slums—their "homes" often were just a sheet of plastic to cover them or a cardboard lean-to against a wall.[8] The urban poverty there seemed much more degrading than the rural poverty of Mozambique.

The people may have been poor materially, but spiritually

the Christians put us to shame! I remember meeting a team of five girls, between fifteen and nineteen years old, who evangelized the villages every weekend. They faced ridicule every time they shared Jesus, but they also risked being beaten up and thrown out of the village. Christians in India are often physically persecuted for their faith. And here I was, too scared to talk to someone about Jesus in a grocery line in the United States!

We were challenged by a number of things we saw and heard in India—like the way a middle-aged housewife started fifty churches in one year[9] or the elderly gentleman who in the first year following his conversion started forty-two churches. Were we just playing at church back home?

We were supposed to be teaching these people how to start churches in their homes. But we were the ones who were really learning, and God was using our own teaching to instruct us! We were also amazed when these Indian Christians believed what we told them. We received several e-mails shortly after we arrived home that said things such as, "Please pray for me. I have started five churches since you were here."

How were we supposed to respond to this? I started to pray. "Lord, I don't have the faith to start fifty churches in a year, but maybe I could have the faith for our little network of churches to grow to ten."

What would God do in response to such a prayer?

He acted quickly. Before we knew it, we were involved in starting six churches simultaneously.

A Mother-in-Law's Wisdom

One church was thanks to Tony's mother. A retired missionary from China, Taiwan, and Hong Kong, she had been living in a retirement community since Tony's father had died. Not long after settling in, she had started a Bible study for the residents. One day she called me.

"Would you be willing to take over my Bible study for me? I'm writing a book and just don't have time to commit to it any longer."

The last thing I wanted to do was run a Bible study in a retirement center. But my mother-in-law is very persistent, and I finally agreed to try it.

After my first week there, I was sold. The ladies were delightful. Some of them knew the Lord, while others were nominal Christians. We shared what was going on in our lives, studied the Bible, and prayed.

"You know, Tony," I said to him after a couple of weeks. "I think this is church. These people live more like the New Testament church than any other church I know. They are literally sharing their lives together on a daily basis. They eat their meals together, and they have far more community than most churches. What do you think?"

"If our definition of church is 'where two or three gather in His name,' then it definitely is church."

"If that really is church, then maybe we should see if any of the other local retirement communities are interested in starting a similar faith community."

A few days later, I went to another retirement home just down the road from our house. "Would you be interested in having a Bible study for the residents here?" I asked the head of the facility. (I intentionally did not use the word *church* in case that would raise a red flag.)

"Why, yes! The old people would love that. When can you start?"

It was that simple. Not only did the staff provide a room, the Bible study was announced over the public address system, and the staff made sure that residents who were interested got to the meeting. After a few weeks, I handed over leadership to an eighty-six-year-old woman from my mother-in-law's retirement center. She ran it until ill health prevented her from doing it, but the group still meets to this day.

Not only did groups start up in retirement homes, but other groups started in offices, neighborhoods, apartment complexes, and low-income housing projects. One group consisted of Catholics who attended Mass on the weekends but came to "real church" on Wednesday nights.

Where Two or Three Friends Gather Together

Our daughter, Becky, a natural evangelist, was a vivacious teen at the time. She wanted to graduate from high school early in order to spend a year with Youth With A Mission (YWAM). YWAM is a Christian mission organization that primarily trains young people and sends them all over the world into mission situations. The Christian school Becky attended did not permit students to graduate early, so she transferred to public school where she befriended many non-Christians.

A few months before she was scheduled to leave for YWAM, one of Becky's new friends from school attempted suicide. When a group of ten girls (including Becky) went to the hospital, Becky learned that in that group only she and one other girl from a Christian family had never tried to kill themselves! Becky wanted to reach these girls before something tragic happened to them. So she invited a group of people over, including these ten, for pizza or a homemade meal each week and we discussed spirituality. Each time we met, we asked one of them to talk about their spiritual journey.

The first week Helen shared her story. Helen had been living with her mother in a different state, but after a particularly heated argument, Helen was shipped off to live with her father and stepmother in Texas. She went from being a cheerleader who knew everyone and did well in school, to knowing no one and struggling academically. During the first few months after the move, she became depressed.

"One day I found myself in the bathroom," she said. "I had all the pill bottles out of the medicine cabinet lined up in front of me and I was about to take them all. But before I did, I cried out, 'God, if there is a God, will You help me?' All of a sudden, I found myself facedown on the floor, and God met me there. Within a couple of days, I met Becky. That was just a few weeks ago."

All of us in the group—even the cool teenage guys—had tears running down our cheeks after Helen had finished. It was easy to talk about Jesus in such an intimate context.

Week after week, a different person told his or her story and we spent time studying the Bible together and praying for each other. The fourteen or more kids who came regularly treated our home as their home. We never knew who we would find sleeping on our couch in the morning!

The night before Becky left for YWAM, we threw a going-away party for her.

"I want to tell more of my friends about Jesus," she said. During the party, she was rebaptized (she had been baptized when she was eight years old) in our hot tub and recommitted her life to the Lord. Fifty of her "closest friends" were there and listened as she told the story of how God was working in her life.

Even after Becky left for YWAM, the kids continued to meet at our home. We often played games like Pictionary with them until late into the night. It was evident when they gave their lives to the Lord because they began to clean up their acts. They stopped drinking and partying every night and eventually asked us if they could get baptized. We did not push them into "praying the sinner's prayer" or "making a decision." But when they asked about baptism, we made sure they understood what it meant and had truly committed their lives to the Lord. Our Jacuzzi became a Jordan River.

As we continued to open our home to these teenagers, we discovered that belonging to the group was extremely important to them—whether they believed in Jesus at the time or not. When we were young, people believed in God first, and then joined a church. But these kids belonged first and immediately entered the discipleship process. Their lives changed, and somewhere in the process, they recognized that they believed in Jesus. We have seen this happen many times since then.

Belonging to the group was extremely important to these teens—whether they believed in Jesus or not.

After a few months, we decided it was time the teens took responsibility for their meetings.

"We could have it at my house," suggested Troy, one of the first of Becky's friends to commit his life to the Lord. He had recently moved in with three other Christians from one of the local churches.

The first night the group met in his home, an entirely new group of people showed up. "I want to learn more about God and giving my life to Him!" announced Katy, one of the newcomers, as she walked in through the door. She gave her life to Jesus that night, and her boyfriend followed a few weeks later. The meeting grew bigger, and two other groups quickly started from it. Everything seemed to be working well with no unforeseen problems.

But when we returned home from another mission trip to India, Troy surprised us with news: "I had to shut down the church."

"Why? What happened?" we asked.

"The youth pastor from the church that my roommates attend heard about what we were doing. He thought someone should be teaching. So one night, he took over the whole thing and started running it himself. I didn't know what to do, and people didn't want to come anymore when he was leading it, so after three weeks, I stopped it." (Tony and I tried to restart the group again, but were unsuccessful.) There were more lessons for us to learn!

Understanding What Church Really Is

While Troy had been trying to hold the house church group together, Tony and I were in India speaking at conferences in several different states. At some of the conferences we shared the platform with an Indian doctor whom God has used mightily to spark a church-planting movement across his region of the country. In 1992, the Lord had instructed him to leave his position as head of a prestigious medical center and plant churches instead. The doctor had no idea how to plant churches, so he studied the Gospels and the book of Acts. As we traveled together, we made sure he was the one who spoke most of the time while we took copious notes. Whenever we had a few moments, we deluged him with questions. We have learned so much from this humble man of God.

"What is a church?" we asked him.

"A church is where two or three meet in Jesus' name," he told us. "But when we used that definition to count the number of churches we had started, the numbers seemed artificially high. We decided that since the Bible often only counts heads of households, we would only count churches with two or three families in them. Then we added other criteria. The 'two or three' must be baptized. [In his particular Indian state, both the person getting baptized and the one doing the baptizing face a three-year jail sentence.] The church has to be led by someone from that village, not an outsider. And finally, we decided that since churches are supposed to multiply, we would only count them if they also birthed another church. Nothing living that God created is supposed to be sterile, and that includes the church!"

"How many churches do you have now?"

"In the past four years, we have seen about 3,500 started," he replied. "Of course, there are thousands more of 'triplet churches,' where two or three are gathered in His name." As of today, several years later, the number of true churches is more than 10,000.

When Becky came back from working with YWAM, she sensed the Lord wanted her to work downtown in the bar district, so she applied for a job as a cocktail waitress. We weren't keen on the idea. Would she be safe? What would our Christian friends think?

But then we were reminded that Jesus was accused of being a "glutton and a drunkard, and a friend of the worst sort of sinners!"[10] If hanging out with sinners wasn't a problem for Him, we trusted the Lord to both take care of and do something through Becky.

Becky had been working for a few months when she asked

if she could have a barbecue at our home for her new friends. Since it was Christmastime, she invited them to a "Baby Jesus Barbecue." (I wondered what people thought we were going to eat!) That evening, close to forty bartenders and bouncers were in our home and another church began. Although the church did not last, several of them became Christians. And other churches were being added all the time.

> Hanging out with sinners wasn't a problem for Jesus.

We decided to begin a monthly Sunday morning celebration for all of the churches. The celebration included a worship team, a full program for kids, and a teaching session, not unlike what you would find in traditional churches. But the celebration ran into some problems.

First, the teens and twentysomethings who recently had become Christians did not do mornings! Added to that, some of the new families who had just become believers hadn't cleaned up their language; the four-letter words used by their kids in everyday speech caused problems for the "nice middle-class" Christian families with kids.

The leadership team (consisting of four couples) sought the Lord and sensed we should stop the regular monthly celebration. "We are modeling traditional church in our celebrations," we concluded. "Let's see what happens if we reduce the number of times we all get together." The decision was made to bring the churches together only if a speaker came to town whom we wanted everyone to have a chance to hear.

We didn't anticipate the effects this change would have.

Quite a number of Christians who had transferred into the network from other churches left to go back to more traditional models of church. In their minds, the monthly celebration was "real" church and the meetings in homes were extra. They wanted Sunday school for their kids and youth programs for their teens. Although they had been out of the traditional church for a while, they still had the traditional church mind-set.

Consequently, the number of churches in our network declined. We were back to working primarily with people who became Christians within the simple church context, plus reaching out to unbelievers.

What Church Really Is

When Jesus was on earth, the main theme of His teaching was the Kingdom of God (Matthew 4:23). Many of His parables illustrated the Kingdom of God (e.g., Matthew 13). Jesus told His disciples to heal people and tell them, "The kingdom of God has come near to you" (Luke 10:9, NKJV). After His resurrection and before His ascension, Jesus spent forty days talking to His disciples about the Kingdom (Acts 1:3).

It's interesting to see that after having spent three years living with Jesus on a daily basis, the disciples lived out what they learned from Him about the Kingdom by meeting together in each others' homes on a daily basis and sharing their lives together (Acts 2:42-47). They called it "church." Could this have been what Jesus modeled for them? Of course! They also met on a daily basis in the

Temple, probably for evangelism, until persecution forced them to scatter (Acts 8:1).

From that point on in Scripture, all the references to church meetings take place in a house—apart from one reference to Paul teaching in the hall of Tyrannus (possibly a school for church planters, since in Acts 19:9-10 Luke says that all of Asia heard the gospel). The first time history indicates that believers met in buildings is in AD 321, when Emperor Constantine adopted Christianity but followed pagan tradition by building special temples for the Christians. A paid, professional clergy class arose.

For a subject so significant to God's Kingdom, it is extraordinary that the word *church (ekklesia)* is mentioned only twice in the Gospels.

In Matthew 16 after Peter's great declaration, "You are the Messiah, the Son of the Living God" (v. 16), Jesus responds, "Upon this rock [i.e., this declaration of truth], I will build my church, and all the powers of hell will not conquer it" (v. 18). This obviously refers to the church universal, made up of all Christians down through the ages, throughout the world. Jesus then goes on: "And I will give you [the church] the keys of the Kingdom of Heaven. Whatever you forbid on earth will be forbidden in heaven, and whatever you permit on earth will be permitted in heaven" (v. 19).

Two chapters later, in Matthew 18:15-17, Jesus describes what should happen if someone sins against another person. First, you confront the person one-on-one. Then you go to the person with one or two witnesses. Finally, if that has no effect, you should tell it to the church. This reference to the church has to refer to a small-group situation.

It would be inappropriate in a megachurch setting or even a large congregation because the person concerned would most likely feel traumatized and leave the church. But in a small group, where relationships are deep and relevant, this kind of action produces results. After all, the purpose of church discipline is to restore the person back to fellowship.

However, it is Matthew 18:18-20 that is the most interesting. Jesus uses the exact same concepts here as He did with the universal church. He says, "Whatever you forbid on earth will be forbidden in heaven, and whatever you permit on earth will be permitted in heaven." Then He adds, "I also tell you this: If two of you agree here on earth concerning anything you ask, my Father in heaven will do it for you. For where two or three gather together as my followers, I am there among them."

In the context of church, Jesus says He is present when two or three are gathered in His name. Many people consider this verse as the primary definition of church.

Church is mentioned in the rest of the New Testament in various other ways. Quite frequently, the descriptive phrase "church in a house" is used. For example, in Romans 16:5, "Give my greetings to the church that meets in their home" refers to the church that met in Priscilla and Aquila's house. This is the outward expression of "where two or three are gathered in My name." The term *church* is also used to describe all of the disciples in a locality, such as a city or region, a group that was probably made up of many smaller groups. Examples of this would be the church at Antioch (Acts 13:1) or the churches of Galatia (1 Corinthians 16:1).

There are three main uses of the word *church* in Scripture: the church in the home (or the church of at least two or three people), the church in a city or region, and the church universal.

However, in our culture, we generally use the word *church* in nonbiblical ways.

- A physical building. When someone says, "I left my Bible at church," everyone knows what the person means—that building with a steeple located at a certain address. But the church is neither a building nor an event.
- A specific denomination. It doesn't matter whether you are a member of a Southern Baptist church or a Roman Catholic church—thinking of your particular denomination when you are talking about the church has a negative effect. The Bible specifically speaks against dividing the body of Christ into different factions (1 Corinthians 1:10-13).
- A specific congregation, such as New Life Church. Again, this is not a biblical use of the term.

So what is a church? The word *ekklesia* that is translated "church" literally means "called-out ones." It was not exclusively a religious term. In fact, elsewhere in the New Testament it is used to describe other kinds of assembly. For example in Acts 19:32, *ekklesia* refers to a rioting mob.

> *The church is who we are 24/7. It is not a place where we go or an activity we do.*

But is church merely a series of weekly meetings? No! Even in simple churches, we have a tendency to refer to it this way. The church is who we are 24/7—a daily experience of living in the Kingdom (Acts 2:46). It is not a place where we go or an event we attend. It is more relational than meeting based. We are members of one another (Ephesians 4:25). Church is about vibrant communities whose common denominator is faith in Christ. Church is a group of disciples relating together in everyday life; when they get together in His name, Jesus Himself is present.

There are several different terms being used to describe this biblical model of church today. Some groups refer to these churches as house churches or home churches. Others refer to them as simple churches or organic churches. These terms refer to a community of God's people who relate together as a small group, loving one another and caring for one another in practical ways. Tony and I personally prefer to use the term *simple church*, because it doesn't imply that the group has to meet in a house. Many of these churches are missional, seeking to multiply by actively reaching into the world of unbelievers or the unchurched around them.

(These simple churches are not reaching out to existing Christians in legacy churches. The last thing we want is for a group of disgruntled Christians to get together and complain about the traditional churches they have left. Why would God multiply that?)

When we view church through these new lenses, our whole understanding changes.

3

THE 10:2b VIRUS

The Men behind a Prayer Movement

These were his instructions to them: "The harvest is great, but the workers are few. So pray to the Lord who is in charge of the harvest; ask him to send more workers into his fields." — LUKE 10:2

✹ From the Day of Pentecost, there has not been one great spiritual awakening in any land which has not begun in a union of prayer, though only among two or three; no such outward, upward movement has continued after such prayer meetings declined.

— A. T. PIERSON

IT IS A breakfast that Kenny remembers as if it happened yesterday. He and his friend John were together at a local restaurant, catching up on each other's lives. Their conversation quickly turned to their shared passion—church planting— and their desire to see a spontaneous, rapid movement of churches planted across their state.

"How are we ever going to see this state saturated with the gospel?" asked Kenny as he took a sip of his coffee. "We know it will take a church-planting movement."

"The real problem is lack of leadership," John observed. "The whole idea of a church-planting movement hinges on an army of men and women church planters. Workers for the harvest are what we really need."

"My modus operandi has always been to enlist seminary students from out of state. If I find someone even half alive, I will suggest, 'Why don't you come to our city and start something?' It's all activity oriented," said Kenny.

"I'm reminded of Luke 10:2, where Jesus tells His disciples that the harvest is ready, and that we should be praying for workers for the harvest," John said.

"Well, I've prayed that prayer in the past when I've been desperate and needed someone to help in a situation."

"Me too."

"But I don't usually keep going. It doesn't take me long before I default to activity. I will pray for a short season, and then I approach someone and say, 'I think God is calling you to do this.' At best, it's just my own effort," confessed Kenny.

"According to the verse in Luke, Jesus says the problem isn't the harvest; it is ripe and ready. The problem is the laborers," said John. "With seventy-two disciples, there were thirty-six church-planting teams. If you add in the original twelve disciples, that would make eighty-four total or forty-two teams! Most churches would be thrilled with that number, but Jesus said it was not enough!"

"What do you suggest we do about it?"

"You know, I think there is something more to this command of Jesus in Luke 10:2 than we realize. And this conversation is more than just our normal complaints about the lack of church leaders. God may be doing something here. Why don't we pray for the next week and see what the Lord is trying to tell us? Then let's get back together and compare notes."

The next week, John and Kenny met again for breakfast.

"You know, as I thought and prayed about it this past week, I had a sense that we need to get together to pray regularly for workers for the harvest," John said.

"I had that same impression," said Kenny. "Do you think we could do it daily?"

"Well, we can't eat breakfast together every day; we're both too busy."

"What if we pray over the phone?"

"Okay, let's try it for a week. If we have the chance to meet together, we'll do it. Otherwise, let's call each other."

Kenny left that meeting feeling somewhat uncomfortable with what he was getting himself into. *This sounds legalistic,* he thought to himself. *I'm really not interested in some kind of formula.* But he had agreed to try it with John, so early the next morning he called him.

"Hi, John. Are you ready to pray?"

"Yes, I'm ready."

"Well, Lord, John and I are here to pray together for workers for the harvest. You tell us that the harvest is ready. We cry out to You for laborers for the harvest in this city. Send us laborers, Lord!"

"And Lord," John continued, "we really don't know how to pray this prayer. Please, will You teach us?"

All went well for a couple of days. But then a day came when they did not connect. When Kenny and John finally got in touch with each other, they decided that if they didn't get through to the other person, the caller would at least leave a voice-mail prayer. It sounded a bit bogus, but they couldn't think of a different solution.

At the end of the first week, John and Kenny met and evaluated what was happening.

"We're enjoying it. Let's just keep doing it and see where it goes."

Kenny had expected that possibly the daily prayer would become ritualistic, but he was surprised—he actually looked forward to their phone calls. The prayers only lasted a few minutes, but the conversation might go longer. Kenny and John shared briefly about their day, caught up with one another's news, and prayed for related concerns. But the main petition was to pray for workers for spiritual harvest.

The weeks of prayer turned into months of prayer, then years of prayer. John and Kenny prayed together virtually every day for five years before they partnered with other prayer warriors.

Effective Prayer

When John and Kenny began praying, they realized that they didn't really know how to pray consistently long-term. How many times can you pray, "Lord, send out workers into Your harvest" before it becomes vain repetition?

"How do we do this, Lord?" they asked.

Reflecting back on this time, Kenny says, "There were two passages that the Lord seemed to impress on us. The first from Luke 18 was the story of an unrighteous judge and a widow seeking justice. The widow kept returning over and over again, asking the judge for justice. When the judge finally gave in to her request, he said, 'I don't fear God or man, but this woman has worn me out!' Jesus said that this is the way all believers are supposed to pray. That encouraged us to be persistent and relentless in our praying.

> How many times can you pray, "Lord, send out workers into Your harvest?"

"Sometimes we would tell Him, 'Well, Lord, here we are again, and we're asking You again for church planters for the harvest.'

"Another thing we learned was to be more specific in what

we ask, and not make a general request. The Greek word for *send* in Luke 10:2 is *ekballo*. The word has an element of violence, of a force that a person cannot resist. It's the same word that is used for casting out a demon! 'Thrust out' or 'throw out' might be more accurate translations. It implies people who are very willing to go. We asked the Lord for people who are already passionate for church planting and have apostolic hearts. God seemed to answer that kind of prayer.

"The idea of specificity came from a story Jesus tells in Luke 11 about a man who asks his neighbor for bread because he has an unexpected visitor and no food to offer him. The man with unexpected company not only asks for bread; he asks for three loaves of bread. That encourages us to be specific in what we ask. For example, we became aware of a community of Russian immigrants in our city and prayed specifically for a worker for those people, and a worker soon contacted us."

Kenny and John soon began to see their prayers answered. In 2002, Kenny was working for the city association of a mainline denomination. (He later moved on to coordinate church planting for that denomination in his state until recently retiring.) Almost immediately, he began getting phone calls, e-mails, or people coming to his office who wanted to start churches in his city. Some of the people were from out of state, but planning to move there. Others were people whom he had known for ten or more years from his city but had not seen for some time. Each worker said the same thing: "I think God is calling me to be involved in church planting."

However, as God answered their prayers, the stereotypical profile of a church planter was about to change. "I used to look for a young, energetic, good-looking, educated, charismatic personality to be a church planter," admits Kenny. "We prayed, 'Lord, help us to recognize these people as they emerge.' Now I see a much broader spectrum of ordinary people God might be calling out for this.

"The results of our prayers were exciting in terms of new church planters," Kenny continues. "But looking back, what really happened was that I changed. To be honest, I never used to believe I was going to get an answer when I prayed. The Lord saved me when I was thirty, and I've been a believer for more than thirty-five years. During that time I've prayed a lot, and the Lord has answered many prayers. But I have never before had that sense of expectancy that comes with a real belief in prayer. Prayer used to be a side issue. Now it has become the focus of my strategy for church planting in this state. I do not have a Plan B. Everything focuses on praying and letting God provide the workers for the harvest.

> "I have never before had that sense of expectancy that comes with a real belief in prayer."

"Another by-product has been the spiritual effect on me. I'm more passionate about prayer than I've ever been. I've seen my personal prayer life take on a new vitality. And I seem to have more hunger for the Word. My wife complains that all I think about these days is church planting. I tell her, 'I really believe I'm more of a missionary now than I've ever been in my life.' That's hard to quantify, but I find that I have more of a burden for the lost, and more interest in the harvest than I've had in twenty years."

The Virus Replicates

"Wouldn't it be amazing if this concept spread to others?" John said one day, a few months into their prayer experiment. "It would be like a virus! People could catch the virus and then infect others with it. Viruses tend to have names that are a combination of numbers and letters, so let's call this one the 10:2b virus since Jesus' command is in the second part of Luke 10:2."

"How do we get other people to join us in prayer? We can't do it by giving away books or creating a program. I think all we can do is tell our stories!"

John and Kenny made a commitment to each other that they would tell their stories at every opportunity, wherever they went. If they had lunch with someone, they shared the virus with them. If they were speaking at a meeting, they talked about it. Their conviction and diligence has grown into a minimovement. All across the United States and in many different countries, people are calling each other daily and praying the 10:2b virus: "Lord, send out laborers into Your harvest." Many people set the alarms on their cell phones to ring at 10:02 in the morning or evening to remind them to pray.

As Kenny and John continued to pray for harvesters, they were also praying that a prayer movement would permeate their state. They have concluded they never will see a true church-planting movement unless it is preceded by a prayer movement.

A typical 10:2b prayer might go something like this: "Lord, we're here again today to thank You for answered prayer in sending harvesters. Thank You for Andrew who contacted me yesterday and who is coming back to this state, interested in church planting. But we're also here today to ask You for more! Give us an army of men and women who are prepared and who don't need a lot of training. Let them have the passion and burden to be involved in church planting and gospel saturation in this state. Lord, we pray for each of the counties in this state. Give us a team of two people who are willing to pray daily for the people in their county."

"We try to keep the prayer primarily focused on the harvest. In the denomination I serve," says Kenny, "prayer meetings usually focus on sick bodies and sad circumstances. 'So-and-so is sick and needs our prayer,' or 'My husband has lost his job.' But the 10:2b prayer is focused on the Kingdom. The effects of praying the virus are beginning to show."

Since they started praying, many people have approached Kenny saying they sense that God wants them to start a church in his state. Some have started individual churches or networks that have thrived. For example, one network led by a seminary professor who started a church in his home has expanded to nearly nineteen churches. One person in his network is reaching out to the urban core of their city, especially to the Goth community. Other churches are reaching out to their neighborhoods with an emphasis on working with kids. Many of the leaders in this network are women. Some of the churches that have started are legacy and some are simple, but they all carry a missional DNA. This network also has begun to work intensively with refugees, particularly the Tibeto-Burman group, the Karen people.

Other churches or networks have floundered, with some of the members going back to legacy churches (although some have since returned to simple church). Why is there difficulty? Many believers from legacy church backgrounds fail to recognize the existence of what has become known as "death valley."[1] When a person is looking from the mountaintop of a legacy church, it is very easy to see the neighboring peak of simple church and assume it is possible to connect a straight line from one to the other.

> Adopting a simple church lifestyle means leaving behind many good things that a legacy church provides.

The reality is that a deep valley exists between the two—death valley. In order to make the journey to a simple church lifestyle, a legacy church believer has to die to many good things that a legacy church provides—good teaching, professional worship, kids' and youth programs. Sometimes it is easier to go back to what you have known than to stay the course of the simple church lifestyle and see its benefits.

However, the long-term results of John and Kenny's prayers are becoming clearer. At a regional level, a thriving network comprising both individual simple churches and smaller networks of churches has emerged. Ten to twelve apostolic men (they are praying for women apostles) pray the 10:2b virus daily, communicate regularly by e-mail, and meet once a month to share stories and pray.[2]

Another outcome is the http://www.lk10.com Web site that John runs. This is a "community of practice" for church planters, with a current membership of five hundred people from twenty-five different countries. The men and women who are regulars to the site post thousands of ideas on how to make disciples and plant churches from their own experiences. They are all committed to praying the Luke 10:2b prayer; how this prayer is being answered around the world is also documented here. The Web site has become a powerful resource for leaders of missional, simple churches.

God delights in answering the 10:2b prayer!

The 10:2b Virus

Kenny and John have seen a prayer epidemic launched. We all know that prayer is the key to seeing God move powerfully. If we really believed it was more than just lip service, would we spend more time on our faces before God?

I recently read an account of an interview with Dr. Paul (David) Yonggi Cho (pastor of the largest church in the world). The interviewer asked what the secret was to his church's explosive growth. He replied that when he first started, it took four to five hours of prayer a day to see God move, but now he has been able to cut down to three hours per day![3]

David Watson, another friend of ours, worked for fourteen years in North India and catalyzed a church-planting movement with more than forty thousand churches. He is now training church planters in Africa who have started more than five thousand churches. David recently surveyed the top one hundred leaders who had produced the most churches to find any common elements in their methodologies. The only common element in every one was the leader's commitment to prayer. These leaders, most of whom also had regular jobs, rose early to spend an average of three hours per day in personal prayer and another three hours in prayer with their teams. They prayed and fasted a day per week and their whole team spent one weekend per month in fasting and prayer.[4]

A few years ago, the International Mission Board of the Southern Baptist Convention identified a new phenomenon occurring in many parts of the world (with the noticeable exception of the Western world). As they studied reports from their missionaries, they observed a spontaneous and rapid—often described as "nearly out of control"—growth in churches started in some areas. This rapid growth was due to conversions, not just Christians transferring from one church to another, resulting in a genuine advance for the Kingdom of God. They called what they saw a "church planting movement," which they define as "a rapid and multiplicative increase of indigenous churches planting churches within a given people group or population segment." For example, in a little more than a decade in Cambodia, the number of Christians increased from around six hundred to more than a hundred thousand.

This is what we are longing for and praying for here, too. We may not be seeing it yet, but the signs point to God doing something unusual. The research of the International Mission Board showed several key, common characteristics in the places that experienced outstanding growth. Prayer is one of these.

This simple church movement needs to be birthed and bathed in prayer. I believe that much of what we are seeing has been initiated by the prayer movement of the last decade or more, thanks to intercessors who have been calling out to God to take His church back. We need people who are willing to spend time before God, crying out for Him to do something far beyond man's best abilities to produce, something that only He can do (and only He will get the credit for). "Unless the LORD builds the house, they labor in vain who build it" (Psalm 127:1, NKJV).

> *Simple church growth has happened thanks to intercessors asking God to take His church back.*

Where are the people who will seek His face hour after hour, pleading with Him for a move of His Holy Spirit to transform this country? Where are the ordinary disciples who are motivated to move out of their comfort zones to preach good news to the poor, comfort the afflicted, and announce freedom to the captives? (Isaiah 61:1).

Am I willing to pay this kind of price? Are you?

4

THE GREAT COMMISSION

The Woman Who Loved Her Neighbors

*I have been given all authority in heaven and on earth. Therefore,
go and make disciples of all the nations, baptizing them in the name
of the Father and the Son and the Holy Spirit. Teach these new
disciples to obey all the commands I have given you. And be sure
of this: I am with you always, even to the end of the age.*
– MATTHEW 28:18-20

☀ Spontaneous expansion [is] the unexhorted and unorganized
activity of *individual members of the church* explaining to others
the Gospel which they have found for themselves. I mean the
expansion which follows the irresistible attraction of the Christian
church for those who see its ordered life, and are drawn to it by
desire to discover the secret of a life which they instinctively desire
to share. I mean also the expansion of the church by the addition of
new churches. I know not how it may appear to others, but to me
this unexhorted, unorganized, spontaneous expansion has a charm
far beyond that of our modern highly-organized missions.
– ROLAND ALLEN, *The Spontaneous Expansion of the Church*

"THE MOMENT I step foot outside my door, I'm in a mission field!" That statement describes how Elizabeth looks at the world as a bold witness for the Lord. But her courage came from great adversity.

When Elizabeth was eight years old, two life-changing events took place. First, after being diagnosed with juvenile diabetes, she spent several weeks in the hospital. That same year, her father and mother separated. Elizabeth's mother had custody of her daughter, but that year during her summer break, Elizabeth stayed with her father.

One summer night he sat her on his lap and said, "Elizabeth, you know I've lost contact with my other kids, but I just want you to know that I love you and I'll never leave you." (Her father had three children by a former wife, but was no longer in touch with them.)

> In her early teens, Elizabeth began partying heavily, trying to fill the void left by her father's absence.

Later that same evening, Elizabeth found her father unconscious, an empty bottle of codeine nearby. It was obviously a suicide attempt. The eight-year-old called her dad's girlfriend.

"Help me, I can't wake Dad."

When the paramedics arrived, Elizabeth was terrified as she watched her father being put in the back of an ambulance to be taken to the hospital. Although her father survived, he was filled with so much guilt and shame that he never contacted Elizabeth again.

When Elizabeth reached her early teens, she began partying heavily, trying to fill the void left by her father's absence. Not surprisingly, she became promiscuous—she longed to be accepted by any male figure. Elizabeth's diabetes got out of control because she refused to take care of herself, causing her to be constantly sick and often hospitalized.

But Elizabeth wasn't alone through these turbulent years. She had three best friends who were there for her. They frequently visited her in the hospital; and after she came home, they spent all their time together. One day the friends were hanging out at her mother's home.

"Let's all go get some coffee," suggested Kylie, Elizabeth's closest friend. "I'll drive."

"No, you can't drive my car," Elizabeth said.

"Oh, let me, please let me," Kylie begged. She kept on until finally Elizabeth threw the keys to her. "Be careful!"

Elizabeth climbed into the passenger seat and put on her seat belt.

"Don't come with me. You go with Jason," ordered Kylie. Kylie wanted Elizabeth to get back with her ex-boyfriend, who was in a truck behind them. Kylie was riding with Elizabeth's two other friends, Amy and Meghan, and another teen named Sarah.

Elizabeth switched cars. She climbed into the front seat of the truck and one of Jason's friends took Elizabeth's place in her car. It was the last time Elizabeth saw her three best friends alive—on the way to the coffee shop Kylie was involved in a horrific accident.

Elizabeth's three best friends were killed instantly, and the other two passengers in the car suffered major injuries. Elizabeth and Jason witnessed the whole thing. For Elizabeth, it was the darkest day of her life, and looking back, she wonders how she ever got through it. Elizabeth struggled with survivor's guilt after the three vibrant girls died. There were many days when she was so sick that she felt there was nothing left to live for.

Over time, by the grace of God, Elizabeth began picking up the emotional pieces of her life again. But her physical problems seemed to get worse.

Possibly as a result of the traumatic shock of seeing her friends killed, Elizabeth developed a peripheral neuropathy, a complication of diabetes that affects the nervous system. She was in constant pain and her weight dropped to seventy-two pounds. Elizabeth was hospitalized again, this time for fifteen months. Although she eventually recovered, she has had to wear leg braces since that time.

Within the next two years, her diabetes caused serious eye problems that required multiple surgeries. The surgery worsened the condition of her right eye; there was so much scar tissue that the retina eventually detached and Elizabeth became blind in that eye. But the sight in her left eye was saved, leaving her with 20/40 vision in that eye. (Overall, she has about 70 percent loss of vision.)

At eighteen, Elizabeth stopped driving because of her poor eyesight. Because she wasn't independent anymore, life completely changed for her. (Elizabeth still thinks she is the most independent person out there. She cannot stand it when people want to help her because she wants to do it on her own!) But God was about to extend His hand to her when, once again, she was hospitalized.

Physical and Spiritual Surgeries

At first, the doctors didn't know what was wrong with her, but blood work eventually showed that her kidneys were failing. She could survive only with dialysis. Elizabeth began spending three days a week at the dialysis center and she was placed on a waiting list for a kidney transplant.

With all this going on, Elizabeth became hungry for God. She found a rapidly growing megachurch and began attending regularly. It didn't take long before she surrendered her life to the Lord, and she matured quickly in her Christian life. For the first time, Elizabeth had a spiritual family— brothers and sisters who cared about her. Marty, one of the assistant pastors at the church, helped her considerably, and Elizabeth, Marty, and his wife, Vicki, became strong friends. Elizabeth didn't let anything keep her from being involved in everything that was going on at church.

More than seven years passed while she waited for a kidney transplant, and Elizabeth's physical condition deteriorated. Finally, doctors told her it would be three more years before she reached the top of the list; the odds of her living that long were low. The doctors advised her to transfer from the kidney transplant list to the kidney/pancreas transplant list. Suddenly, she was number one on the list! Although the change involved more challenges, it could save her life. Two months later, she had the double transplant.

There were complications with the new pancreas, and Elizabeth had three surgeries during that first year before it was working normally. Her recovery took eighteen months. But with her new pancreas, Elizabeth didn't have to take insulin for the first time in twenty-three years! (The pancreas is the organ that produces insulin.) That alone was a gift.

Elizabeth became even more active in church. She loved intercessory prayer and worship and always helped wherever she was needed. She had a heart for those who did not know Jesus, taking teams to the local shopping center to minister to the Goths who hung out there. The Lord touched many people through her life.

But problems surfaced in the megachurch. People started to leave when major moral issues in the leadership came to light. Marty and Vicki, one of the couples who left, were gaining a vision for simple churches. They were excited about the possibilities of evangelism within a multigenerational home context. (In all, seven other churches started from the breakup of this megachurch, two of which are networks of simple churches.)

Exciting Changes

When Marty and Vicki left the church, they birthed a new church called The River that Elizabeth joined. Her desire was to have a home one day that she could open up to broken and lost people. She dreamed of having a church meet in her home.

"When I am married, and there is spiritual leadership in my home, I will open it up to those in need," Elizabeth said.

The River met in another church's building. Scott, a young man from that church, was always working on the sound system when Elizabeth arrived early to prepare for worship. Like Elizabeth, Scott loved God with all his heart. He and Elizabeth got to know each other, fell in love, and a year later they were married.

When Elizabeth and Scott moved into his home in a mobile home park, they prayed, "Lord, if You want us to open our home to others, please show us how." A few months after their wedding, Scott and Elizabeth attended a house church conference where they heard about simple ways of starting churches with unbelievers.

"Prayer-walk in your neighborhood," the speaker said. "Trust the Lord to bring you to a person of peace."

> "Lord, if you want us to open our home to others, please show us how."

This was the first time they had heard Luke chapter 10 taught so intensively. "We can do this," they said to each other. They weren't going to wait for Marty to help them or for The River to give them permission to start something. From that point on, they owned the vision. Marty encouraged them to do something about it.

A couple of evenings later, Elizabeth and Scott made their first prayer-walk. What made it unusual was that Elizabeth had a broken foot and actually couldn't walk. So Scott pushed her in a wheelchair around the mobile home park. Sometimes they prayed out loud for their neighbors; other times they prayed quietly to themselves. Sometimes the Lord stirred their hearts to pray for things they knew were going on in the various homes.

Because Scott had lived in the mobile home park for a number of years, he knew most of the residents by name. He gardened and often would help people. For years he had been praying and planting the seeds of Christ's love in his neighbors' lives. And people noticed a radiance about him.

Scott and Elizabeth were completing their circuit of the park when someone called out.

"Hi, Scott!"

There, in a carpeted carport, sat a neighbor. Janet was relaxing in a chair with a bottle of beer in her hand.

"Hi, Janet," Scott said. "How're you doing?"

"Sit down, sit down! Visit with me." It was clear that she was excited to see them. "Oh, let me get you a beer. Do you want a beer?"

"Oh, that's okay, Janet. Don't worry."

"Oh no, no, no. I'll get you a beer!"

As Janet disappeared into her mobile home, Scott and Elizabeth remembered the passage in Luke 10 where Jesus told His disciples to eat and drink whatever is set before them.

"Just receive it," they heard the Lord whisper to them.

Elizabeth looked at Scott; they knew that offering a beer

to someone was Janet's way of showing hospitality. They would receive it with a smile!

"Thanks, Janet."

Janet felt comfortable with Scott and Elizabeth because they didn't act holier than her. They listened to her and loved her. She was a lonely lady who wanted company. She talked about her life while they drank half a beer!

As they were leaving, Elizabeth noticed Janet's large vegetable garden with an abundant crop of ripening tomatoes and peppers.

"Oh, Janet, your vegetable garden is so beautiful. I'd really like to have one too. Can you help me? Would you like to come over for dinner one night?"

"Sure, I can do that."

A few days later, Janet came to dinner, and the friendship among the three neighbors began to deepen.

> **Scott and Elizabeth didn't act "holier than thou" with Janet.**

The Lord started to lead Scott and Elizabeth to others. Several times, at the Lord's leading, they knocked on a person's door and when the door opened would greet the one who answered with, "Hello, I'm your neighbor!" Other times as they were walking around the mobile home park, Elizabeth and Scott saw people watering their yards and they would stop and talk with them. They greeted whomever they met at the mailbox. Whenever the opportunity arose, they invited neighbors over for dinner.

Janet helped Elizabeth plant a vegetable garden where Elizabeth planted one plant for every neighbor who came to her home for dinner. She lovingly tended the plants and prayed for her neighbors.

"Lord, just as You are making this plant grow, will You help the person this plant represents grow in their relationship with You?"

After a few weeks, Scott and Elizabeth decided to host a neighborhood dinner. "We'll invite all the people we've had contact with over the last few weeks," Elizabeth said to Scott. "And we'll see what the Lord does."

When The River heard what they were doing, they gave Scott and Elizabeth one of their "church-in-a-box" kits, with paper plates, cutlery, and a dry-erase board. Some members of The River had qualms about giving the house church tote kit to a couple who were just inviting non-Christians over for dinner. "Is it really a church if they are not all saved?" they asked.

"We don't *go* to church; we *are* the church," Marty responded. "If church is where two or three are gathered in His name, then Scott and Elizabeth are the church. Jesus is going to be there, God will be moving by His Holy Spirit, and people are going to be discipled."

Eating and Meeting

When Janet came to the first neighborhood dinner, she brought her friend Jean. Jean walked in, clutching a big bottle of red wine, with Janet behind her, carrying a twelve-pack of beer in a grocery bag. After the meal, everyone was sitting in the living room, when Janet accidentally spilled a beer on their brand-new carpet.

"I'm so sorry, I'm so sorry!" Janet could not apologize enough. Scott ran to get some rags to clean it up.

"Janet, look at me!" Elizabeth said to her. "I care about you more than I care about this carpet. This carpet can be replaced, but you can't." Janet stared at Elizabeth as if she were speaking a foreign language. Janet obviously had never heard such loving words before. From that moment, Janet's life started to change because she experienced the unconditional love of God through Elizabeth. Janet never brought beer to Scott and Elizabeth's home again.

Elizabeth is bold in her outreach. "If I see someone who's broken or hurting, I think to myself, *Do I go home and pray about this or do we do something about it?* I'm one of those people who like to do something. I think we're mistaken if we hear about a need and think all we need to do is pray. We do need to pray—a lot! But when God puts a need right in front of us, we need to do more than just pray about it.

> Janet's life started to change because she experienced the unconditional love of God through Elizabeth.

"That's why we had a neighborhood dinner. The first time, we didn't ask our guests to bring anything. Many of the people in the mobile home park live on Social Security, and they don't have a lot to offer. What's so neat is watching the spiritual growth that occurs naturally around the dining-room table.

"It's an ongoing process. Janet is a good example. There have been so many changes in her life that I believe she has become a follower of Jesus, even though she may not recognize it yet. She comes from a Jehovah's Witness background. When we started, Scott and I did all the praying. But now Janet gives thanks for the food. This is a big step for her. She thanks the Lord for good neighbors and friends who are part of her life.

"At Christmas, the Salvation Army gave Janet a gift basket that contained a complete turkey dinner. She wanted us to have it for our neighborhood meal. We didn't want to take it from her because she has so little. But God spoke to us and said, 'She wants you to receive it!' She was so excited to share it with all of us. It was the first time she had ever contributed to the meal."

Scott and Elizabeth pray together before each of the neighborhood meals, asking that God will be glorified in what goes on. When people arrive, they all hold hands and bless the food before sharing in the meal together. Most of the ministry happens around the dining table. People share what is going on in their lives, and they talk about a passage from the Bible. They end their time together by praying for each other.

Another woman named Katie has also changed since meeting the couple at a dinner. Katie suffers from the effects of a head injury she sustained in an accident years ago. Katie's family members don't have the patience to listen to her talk because her speech has been affected by the injury. Katie is distressed by her condition, but Elizabeth is able to relate to her.

"Why am I here? Can God use me?" Katie asked.

"Katie, the Lord wants to use you despite your trials and challenges. Whatever disabilities you have, God wants to use you. This is what happened to me. God wants to use you as much as He wants to use me. And He wants to use you in a powerful way. Isn't that wonderful?"

"I don't really understand why, but it's still cool. I help Billie next door take out her trash because she has a walker and she can't take it out herself."

"Well, there you are. God is using you to minister to your neighbors."

"And I take Cindy's trash out too, because she doesn't feel good. I take out her trash and Billie's trash and my trash. And I help Barbara when she needs things done around her house."

"You see, the Lord is showing you how He's using you!"

Katie and Elizabeth have now been meeting one-on-one for some time. Katie is ready to be baptized, and the whole simple church will attend that celebration.

All the adversity Elizabeth has endured in her life has transformed her into a strong and resolute woman of God. She loves to tell people about Jesus. The moment she steps out her front door, she considers it an opportunity to talk with others about Him. Even those times when Elizabeth is hospitalized due to complications from her transplant, she knows God has a divine appointment waiting for her there. No matter who she meets or what that person is going through, Elizabeth can identify with them and encourage them because of the challenges she has faced in her life. If the person is ill, she shares and prays with her. If the person has suffered a loss, she ministers to the person's grief. No matter where she goes, there is some kind of ministry waiting for her.

"Your neighbor is not just the person who lives next door. It can be the person in the hospital bed next to you, or the one beside you in the line in the grocery store," Elizabeth says. "That person could die tomorrow. What are we waiting for? The great commission means that we slow our lives down enough to see the ministry that is right in front of us. It's so simple, yet we make it so complicated."

> The great commission means slowing our lives down enough to see the ministry that is right in front of us.

Scott and Elizabeth continue to be amazed at how God works so simply and supernaturally as they care for the people around them. They persist in seeking God's will and counsel for the next step. Scott and Elizabeth know that obedience is the key to seeing the glory of God in their neighborhood, and they are determined to follow the great commission.

The Great Commission

The great commission is the "great omission" in most churches today.

In the great commission (Matthew 28:18-20), Jesus commands His disciples, "Go and make disciples of all nations, baptizing them in the name of the Father and of the Son and of the Holy Spirit, teaching them to obey everything I have commanded you. And surely I am with you always, to the very end of the age" (NIV).

The great commission is not a "take it or leave it" option for Christians. Many of us live in self-made Christian ghettos, never developing meaningful relationships with unbelievers. We believe that friendship with people in the world will somehow contaminate us. We avoid relationships of any depth with people outside the church and often are so busy with Christian activities that we have no time for others. It gets to the stage where we don't know how to relate with non-Christians other than inviting them to a meeting. People see straight through our motives when we make them "projects" rather than developing authentic friendships with them.

In the book *unChristian,* David Kinnaman explores the issue of what a new generation really thinks about Christians. His research sadly concludes that Christians are seen as antihomosexual (91 percent of "outsiders"), judgmental (87 percent), and hypocritical (85 percent).[1]

> Many of us never develop meaningful relationships with unbelievers.

But the apostle Paul says in Romans 10:14, "How can they hear . . . unless someone tells them?"and in Matthew 11:19, Jesus was called a friend of sinners. No, not all of us are evangelists, but all of us are to be witnesses to what Jesus has done in our lives (Acts 1:8). We have the life of Jesus within us. If we ask the Lord for opportunities to share that life with others, He will be delighted to answer that prayer.

DNA is the genetic code contained in all the cells of a person's body that is copied and passed down from generation to generation. Healthy DNA is essential for a body to function and reproduce. It is the same in the body of Christ. We need healthy DNA for reproductive Kingdom life.

Our friend Neil Cole has described the DNA of organic church as

Divine truth: truth from God seen in both the person of Jesus Christ and the Scriptures.

Nurturing relationships: God is relational and has created us as social creatures with an intrinsic need for relationships.

Apostolic mission: God sends us as His representatives to make disciples of all nations.[2]

In most of our simple churches, divine truth and nurturing relationships come fairly naturally. However, apostolic mission as given to us in the great commission (Matthew 28:18-20) and in John 20:21 ("As the Father has sent me, so I am sending you") presents us with the greatest challenge.

In the great commission Jesus gives us four directives:

We are to go. In most churches, even in our simpler expressions of church, we ask people to *come*: "Come to our special meeting; come to hear this incredible speaker!" Essentially, we are asking people to cross a huge cultural divide by coming to our religious meetings where we get them to sit down and stand up, sing songs they don't know, and then give their lives to Christ. All of those things are totally foreign to them. Praise God that many people do give their lives to Him in just that way. However, Jesus instructed us to go to them. We are to get out of our comfort zones, cross the barriers into their culture, and touch them in a way that is relevant to them. Despite her immense physical obstacles, Elizabeth chooses to live this way.

We are to make disciples of all nations. What is a nation? In all of our cities there are different segments of society that are basically untouched by church or the gospel (see Josh's story in chapter 5). We should be seeking the Lord on behalf of these people. How do we make disciples of these groups? We are looking for far more than a person deciding to follow Christ and praying to be saved from hell.

We are to make disciples, not mere converts. We are seeking a radical life change, a whole new way of living. How will we know when a nation has been discipled? When that people group or subculture is multiplying churches with indigenous (local) leaders without needing outside help.

We are to baptize the new believers. George Patterson was a missionary and church planter for many years and now mentors church planters. He has researched the subject of baptism and has found that the dropout rate of new converts on the mission field is normally around 95 percent. However, this plummets to near zero if people are baptized quickly. (Obviously there may be reasons to delay baptism, such as sickness or waiting for the river to thaw. The important thing is that baptism is not seen as something that has to be "earned.")

In the New Testament, people were baptized on the same day that they repented and committed their lives to the Lord. For example, on the Day of Pentecost, the three thousand new converts were baptized immediately (Acts 2:41). There is no scriptural precedent for delaying baptism until a person has been through the church's Christianity 101 program!

In many nations where people are persecuted for becoming followers of Jesus there are few, if any, repercussions if a person merely says that he has become a Christian. But when he or she is baptized, all hell breaks loose! It's as if Satan recognizes the strategic nature of baptism, even if we don't. Baptism is a rite of passage between a person's old life and his or her new life in Christ (Romans 6:3-5). It is far more than just a step of obedience or an opportunity to witness to friends.

Baptism is far more than just a step of obedience or an opportunity to witness to friends.

We are to teach new disciples to obey Jesus' commands—not just learn about them. It's important for a new Christian to learn early on to obey the will of God as soon as he or she understands it, whether it is from the written Word or from hearing the voice of the Lord in his or her heart (Romans 8:14). That will then become a foundation in the person's Christian walk that will last the rest of his or her life.

In Romans 15:16, the apostle Paul writes, "I bring you [the Gentiles] the Good News so that I might present you as an acceptable offering to God." God is pleased when we "offer" Him the new disciples we have won to Christ.

Elizabeth is committed to living out the great commission where she lives. She seizes every opportunity she can with a daring, reckless faith to tell others the Good News and her life is bearing much fruit. If Elizabeth can do it, so can we!

5

BEARING MUCH FRUIT

The Troubled Teen Whose Life Made a Difference

So now there is no condemnation for those who belong to Christ Jesus. And because you belong to him, the power of the life-giving Spirit has freed you from the power of sin that leads to death.
— ROMANS 8:1-2

⚙ Most Christians today are trying to figure out how to bring lost people to Jesus. The key to starting churches that reproduce spontaneously is to bring Jesus to lost people. We are not interested in starting a regional church, but rather in making Jesus available to a whole region.

— NEIL COLE, *Organic Church*

FROM AN EARLY age John and Gloria knew their son, Josh, was different from his siblings.

When Josh was five years old, Gloria got a call from a friend. "I was just at the shopping center and I saw Josh there alone."

"What! You must be mistaken," replied Gloria. "Josh is in his room playing."

But when Gloria and John looked, he wasn't there. In fact, Josh was nowhere to be seen—in or out of the house. When John noticed that his son's little bicycle was missing, the two of them rushed down to the shopping center a mile away. Sure enough, there he was!

"Josh, what are you doing?" they asked him.

"I want to buy a compass with that dollar Nana gave me," he replied.

"How did you get across the highway?"

"A man helped me cross the road."

"Josh, you let a stranger help you across the road?"

"Oh, he wasn't a stranger," Josh said. "You always tell me, 'Don't get into a car with strangers,' and he wasn't in a car!"

One Christmas Eve when Josh was seven years old, Gloria noticed her young son crying as he headed to his room. "What's wrong, Josh?"

"I killed that turkey!" he kept repeating. Gloria thought he was referring to the turkey meal they had just eaten.

"What turkey are you talking about?" But she couldn't make any sense out of what he was saying.

Later that evening, when all the guests were gone, she went back to console Josh.

"Josh, what happened?" she asked.

The neighbors' domestic turkey had escaped from its run and flew over the fence into their yard. Josh saw it and wanted to help because the neighbors were out of town for the holidays. So Josh asked John if he could use his snake catcher; Josh planned to catch the turkey by the neck and lead it back to the neighbor's yard.

On Christmas morning, John and Gloria found the enormous white turkey lying dead in their neighbors' front yard across the street.

"Oh my gosh, John!" exclaimed Gloria. "He did kill a turkey. John, get that turkey out of here!"

On one memorable Thanksgiving when John tried to start a fire in the fireplace, the house filled with smoke. Something seemed to be jammed in the chimney because the damper wouldn't open. Dousing the smoldering wood, John waited until the next day to investigate. John and a friend found Coke bottles, cinder blocks, and other debris— a whole wheelbarrow full of things Josh had dropped down the chimney. It wasn't a malicious prank; eight-year-old Josh, wanting to be helpful, was trying to kill some birds that had flown into the chimney. He had succeeded.

"I have a whole new respect for Josh," said John. "Anyone who could haul that much stuff onto the roof and drop it down the chimney has to have some strength."

But as Josh got older, his antics took a darker turn. Josh

was constantly in trouble because his "good intentions" always seemed to backfire on him. Once, Josh shot all the neighbor's windows out with his BB gun—he was trying to pick off wasps from the nests under the eaves of the house. Focused on taking care of the problem, Josh was quite unaware of the destruction he was causing.

John and Gloria were always careful not to leave him alone at home. If they did, either the police or the fire department would be waiting for them when they returned. One time Josh called 911 just to see if the number worked! It did, and the fire truck came!

> **From the moment he was born, Josh was troubled.**

It became apparent that Josh marched to a different drumbeat. He was a good-looking kid, but he just didn't fit in because of his erratic behavior. From the moment Josh was born, he was troubled, and it took a toll on his close family. He pitted one family member against another. Josh could see what other people's weaknesses were and then use those weaknesses to control them. One of those people was his mother, Gloria, whom he combated most often. Counselors told Josh's parents that this was common with kids like Josh.

His uncanny ability to know things about people—if they were real or not—was one of the problems Josh had with church; he sensed the hypocrisy. One of Gloria's friends described Josh, saying, "He's like an old soul; he just knows things!"

Life at school was no different. Josh's disruptive behavior continually landed him in trouble. School officials called Gloria almost every single day during every school year except when Josh was in eighth grade. That year, Josh had a male teacher whom he respected. The teacher showed Josh tough love, and Josh made straight A's. That was the one and only year he did well.

John and Gloria's lives became an emotional and terrifying roller coaster with Josh.

Reaching Out to Throwaway Kids

At seventeen, Josh was placed in a special education program on the campus of an alternative school. One day he announced to John and Gloria that he was a member of a gang. John and Gloria didn't believe him. But soon they discovered that Josh was friends with all the gang members who attended the alternative school.

When Josh's academic problems surfaced in the alternative school, Gloria started homeschooling him. It wasn't long before kids from the neighborhood began coming to their house. Gloria couldn't believe the number of "throwaway kids" who showed up. These kids, twelve years old and older, weren't skipping school; they had been weeded out of the school system because of their behavior problems. The kids loved to hang out at John and Gloria's house because they knew they were welcome there.

It was about this time that John and Gloria got involved

in a home church. Every Sunday evening they carpooled with others and made the hour-long journey to a church that met in the home of Mike and his wife. Once or twice Josh went with his parents. Gloria believed that the attraction for Josh was his sense that the people who were part of that little church were not playing games; they lived what they said.

> The kids knew they were welcome at John and Gloria's house.

Throughout his life, Josh never showed much interest in spiritual things. The only reference to his beliefs that Gloria heard him make was, "I believe in God, and I also believe in the other guy. But I don't want anything to do with him [Satan]."

One Sunday afternoon Gloria was in the kitchen fixing a dish to take to church. Quite a few of the "throwaway kids" had been hanging around the house all weekend with Josh. Some of the girls came into the kitchen.

"What's that?" they asked, watching Gloria spoon cake mix into a pan.

"We are going to home church and this is for our potluck dinner," she replied.

"Can we go?"

"Sure, you can come with us."

"Well, what should we wear?" asked one of the girls.

"It doesn't matter what you wear. Wear what you have on!"

"Can we go right now?"

Gloria called Mike. "Are you ready for this? We're bringing gang members to church tonight!"

Cramming Josh and as many of the kids as they could into the van, they drove to the meeting. All the kids seemed to enjoy it, only temporarily distracted when Josh walked up and down the stairs and made weird noises.

A few days later, Josh surprised Gloria with a question. "Can we have one of those potlucks at our house?"

"Well, I guess so," she replied, guessing that he was talking about church.

Gloria called Mike. "Would you be willing to meet with these kids up here?" she asked.

"Well, yes! If they want to, I'll come and be with them."

Finally two months later, a Sunday afternoon was open for everyone. During the week Gloria kept asking Josh, "Are your friends going to come or not?" But Josh couldn't say for sure whether anyone would or not.

At 5:00 p.m., some of the kids showed up at the house. Gloria called Mike to let him know.

"Hold them off. Order some pizza and I'll come right away," he said.

When Mike arrived, everyone gathered on the patio to eat and then talk about the Bible. Mike told the kids they could ask him anything; the kids opened up because they sensed Mike was sincere and nonjudgmental. As he was leaving, a number of the kids told Mike that they wanted to meet with him again sometime.

Unless a Kernel of Wheat . . .

Two days later Jimmy, a friend of Josh's oldest brother, Monty, telephoned Gloria several times from a motel. Gloria knew Jimmy was an alcoholic and hearing the desperation in his voice, she persuaded him to tell her his room number. She felt she needed to act quickly—Jimmy's brother had committed suicide in a hotel room a few years before. Gloria picked up Josh and three of his friends and found herself driving past the motel where Jimmy was staying.

"I want to check on Jimmy—he sounded really bad," she told Josh. She pulled into the parking lot and hurried to his room. The door wasn't locked; Jimmy was sitting on the bed with a noose around his neck.

Gloria rushed over to him.

"Jimmy!" she cried, pulling the noose over his head.

"My life is so useless!" he sobbed.

Gloria did not know what to say so she just sat with her arm around Jimmy's shoulders.

Suddenly Josh barged into the room, upset because he had been left sitting in the car. But instantly, he perceived what was going on. As he walked across the room, Gloria looked at him and thought, *Who is this?* Josh's countenance had totally changed. He walked over to Jimmy and put a hand on his shoulder.

"It's going to be okay, man," he said. Then turning to Gloria he said, "Mom, go home and get Dad. I'll stay here with Jimmy."

"Josh spoke with such authority that I just did it," Gloria later recalled. "I was so amazed because he never did anything responsible. I went home, got John, and we drove back to the motel. When we arrived, Josh and Jimmy were standing out front, laughing. I thought, *I can't believe this. I can't believe Jimmy looks like this!*

On the way back home, Josh had another surprise. "Jimmy and I talked. Jimmy doesn't want me to end up like him. So I've made up my mind I'm going to quit smoking. I'm going to enroll in college, but tomorrow I'm going to mow the yard and show Dad I can be responsible."

Sitting behind John in the backseat, Gloria's surprised look met his in the rearview mirror.

What's going on? thought Gloria. *Josh is seventeen years old and I've never heard him say anything like this before. He never does anything to please us. He's just not that kind of person. I can't believe I'm hearing him say these things! It's as if he's repenting for what he's done.*

That evening, Josh and seven or eight of his friends were watching TV in his bedroom, a room John had created from their garage.

> **Josh found the gun his dad kept in his vehicle.**

Gloria was out having a cup of coffee with a friend. John had taken Jimmy home and then gone to bed early. While John was sleeping, Josh crept into his parents' bedroom and took his father's car keys. Josh unlocked the car and found the gun his dad kept in the vehicle.

In his bedroom, Josh carefully unloaded the gun and

pocketed all the bullets. (He had been taught how to handle guns.) He pointed the gun at the TV screen and pulled the trigger. *Click.*

"Quit doing that, Josh!" said one of the girls. "Your dad's going to get up and find you with that gun, and you'll be in big trouble!"

But Josh loved showing off. He kept playing with the gun, pointing it at one thing, then another, pulling the trigger each time.

"Quit it, Josh!"

Josh flopped down on the couch. There was an explosion and Josh slumped backward.

"Josh, now look what you've done!" The other kids thought he had fired a shot into the ceiling, and that he was acting like he was hit to scare them. Actually, when Josh fell backward on the couch with the gun in his hand, his elbow hit the arm of the couch so hard that it dislodged a bullet stuck in the gun barrel. The gun fired and the bullet went through Josh's forehead.

As soon as they realized what happened, the kids freaked out. They ran out of the garage to the front door and rang the doorbell, waking John.

"Josh shot himself," they cried.

When Gloria got home, the street was filled with police cars and ambulances. John was standing alone in the front yard.

Oh, no! What's Josh done now? I hope he hasn't hurt anyone.

As Gloria stepped out of the car, John came up to her, tears running down his cheeks.

"Josh is gone!" he said.

Gloria started to cry. She wasn't surprised that her son's life had ended like this. He had caused them so much grief, yet now his life was tragically over.

In the middle of the night, Gloria called to let Mike and his wife know what had happened. Mike shared what the Lord clearly spoke through the Scriptures.

"Unless a grain of wheat falls into the earth and dies, it remains alone; but if it dies, it bears much fruit."[1]

"Lord, bring Your glory out of this terrible situation," they prayed.

That night, John and Gloria talked. They knew too many couples whose marriages had been destroyed by personal tragedies. They decided they would not let Josh's death break them apart. There would be no "what if" or "if only"—no one was to blame for what had happened. (Their relationship has actually grown closer since Josh's death.)

> "The only thing that would make sense of Josh's death is if some of his friends find the Lord."

John and Gloria asked Mike to speak at Josh's memorial service a few days later.

"We'd like you to present the gospel and invite people to accept Jesus," they told him. "The only thing that would make any sense out of Josh's death is if some of his friends find the Lord."

. . . Bearing Much Fruit

When fifty or more members of several different gangs marched into the church building for the service, one of the church members became distraught. "We can't have these kids here. They don't belong. Suppose they start fighting or breaking things up. They need to wait outside!"

"These kids are where they need to be. These are the kind of kids who need to be in church," another member reassured her.

The gang members were well behaved during the service. John and Gloria learned later that Josh had been a member of all of the gangs represented, always trying to negotiate peace among them. Mike told everyone there that Josh's last wish was that his friends would come to the "potluck Bible study" because he cared about their spiritual lives. "The only thing that would make sense of his death is if you would give your lives to Jesus," he said to them during the service. Twenty-eight kids—including Jimmy—responded! Each one signed a piece of paper so that John and Gloria could follow up with them. Gloria still has that piece of paper and considers it one of her most treasured possessions.

As the gang members filed out of the church, each one handed Gloria a rose.

What a nice gesture for them to bring me flowers! Gloria thought. She did not realize at the time that if a gang member dies, it is customary for the other members of the gang to each put a rose on the casket. Since there was no casket, they all gave their flowers to Gloria!

The gang members asked John and Gloria if there could be a potluck in memory of Josh. The following Sunday more than fifty gang members crowded into John and Gloria's living room, leaving their gang colors and hatred for each other outside.

But it wasn't a one-time event. Week after week the kids came, and each week more of them gave their hearts to Jesus. (John and Gloria estimate that around a hundred kids eventually became Christians.) As their lives were transformed, their behavior also changed. Gloria remembers one kid saying, "I was really annoyed by someone this week, but instead of beating him up, I just walked away."

John and Gloria knew that they were witnessing a miracle firsthand because the gangs in that particular city were renowned for violence and crime.

Josh's Wish Realized

One of the first gang girls to become a Christian was Shaker's girlfriend. "Shaker" was a gang leader who had been arrested and was in a Christian-based rehabilitation center. He accepted the Lord there and he and his girlfriend wrote to each other, telling the exciting things the Lord was doing.

When Shaker was released, he joined the Bible studies. Attendance thinned out when he arrived—only Shaker's gang came now because rival gang members were forbidden.

At Christmas, the kids gave John and Gloria an ornament in their gang colors—pink and black—to show their acceptance.

Mike led the potlucks every week until an ex–gang member who had become a Christian years before approached John and Gloria. Bobby had been a Satanist until Jesus radically changed his life. He had a heart for kids from gang backgrounds. The first time he came to a potluck and saw what the Holy Spirit was doing, he could hardly contain himself. Mike asked Bobby to lead the group when he wasn't able to, and eventually let the former gang member take his place.

John and Gloria stayed involved, taking the kids on two retreats. The second one was the most memorable. The retreat leaders had spent much time in prayer beforehand and had their own preconceived ideas about what God would do. The whole weekend was chaotic; the kids were rebellious and out of control. When they returned home, Shaker took action: he threw one of the worst troublemakers out of the gang and sent the others to apologize to John and Gloria. It was a touching scene—one by one, each gang member knelt at Gloria's feet and told her specific things that gang member appreciated about Gloria.

"Thank you for the Easter baskets you prepared for us. We're sorry for the way we acted."

"Thank you for driving us to the retreat."

They did the same to John.

"We felt so humbled," Gloria remembers. "We were amazed at the integrity of the kids. We had expected and hoped for some kind of religious fervor from the weekend. It could have been just an emotional experience, but the results were far more lasting. These kids live such harsh lives that they didn't respond to our taking them away the same way other kids would. Shaker showed them how they had erred and that they had to repent for the way they acted and learn to appreciate what we had done for them. The retreat did not accomplish what we had hoped for and yet the lesson they learned was far more valuable." She laughs. "I'll never forget those big, tough gang members carrying around their Easter baskets!"

As the kids became Christians, they stopped coming to the potlucks. Because this was a gang Bible study, when they were no longer gang members, they just didn't show up. Some of them became involved in local churches. Josh's friendship had brought them to faith in Jesus. The young man who had tried his parents' patience all his life was a seed that literally fell to the ground and died, producing a great harvest.

Much Fruit

Now when someone asks Gloria about Josh, her answer reveals years of reflection.

"Why did God allow us to have a child like that? We spent every moment trying to help him, and then he was gone. We learned so much through dealing with him. God uses all kinds of things to teach us and to grow us into what He wants us to be. Life is a tapestry and Josh was a part of ours. I don't know if Josh could have ever functioned as a normal adult. Maybe that's why the Lord allowed this."

Some of the kids still stay in touch with Gloria and many of their lives remain changed. One of them has even gone into ministry.

"We found out after Josh died that he did a lot of loving things for people that we never knew about. And then look at what God did through his death! All these kids' lives changed because of Josh. God was incredibly glorified through Josh's death. I want his story to live on and to continue to bear fruit—that's the greatest memorial he could have."

It is difficult for people like Josh and his friends to get involved in legacy churches. They find the services boring and irrelevant. Many legacy churches are uncomfortable including kids whose language is offensive and whose behavior is unpredictable. They do not fit into a stereotypical middle-class church culture. But that feeling of not being able to fit in doesn't only apply to people like Josh. Increasingly, Christianity is seen as unimportant in people's lives. The church is no longer where they turn when they have a need.

The attractional model of church ("Come and hear our special speaker") is not the most effective way to reach those who need to hear the gospel message. Think of it this way. Water can exist as both a liquid and a solid. An attractional model of church is like ice—not in the sense of God's "frozen chosen," but because it exists at a certain time in a certain place. However, if you encourage people to get out of the building (whether it is a building with a steeple or a building with a chimney) and reach out to those around them, you are melting the ice. The result-ing water—the Good News of the Kingdom—will seep into every crack and crevice of society. This is liquid church.[2]

The great commission (Matthew 28:18-20) tells us that we are to make disciples of all nations. What are nations? The word *nations* translates the Greek words *ta ethne*, from which we get our word *ethnic*. So the idea of nations is people groupings or subcultures that are distinct seg-ments of society, each with their own culture, language, and customs.

For example, in our city there are many different sub-cultures: students, skaters, yuppies, the elderly, mall rats, and club kids, as well as people from different nationali-ties and the poor, to name just a few. Some subcultures have easy access to the gospel while others, like Josh and his gang friends, are quite isolated from it. Although our city has many churches, their mem-bers are primarily white, middle-class families. Sadly, the majority of the other subcultures no longer darken the doors of churches. The best person to reach them is usually someone from their own cultural group.

> *Unreached groups of all ages will respond to genuine overtures of friendship.*

Unreached groups of all ages need true meaning in their lives. Given the opportunity, they will respond to gen-uine overtures of friendship. But if they feel that they are one-time targets for preaching the gospel, these groups on the fringe of society will see right through us. We need to open our eyes and see the opportunities the Lord has placed around us and then take action!

6

LUKE 10 PRINCIPLES

The Woman with a Heart as Big as Texas

When you enter a house, first say, "Peace to this house." If a man of peace is there, your peace will rest on him; if not, it will return to you. Stay in that house, eating and drinking whatever they give you, for the worker deserves his wages. Do not move around from house to house. When you enter a town and are welcomed, eat what is set before you. Heal the sick who are there and tell them, "The kingdom of God is near you." — LUKE 10:5-9, NIV

☀ In His economy, God has already planted persons of peace in every human habitation, be it a city, a village or a neighborhood (Acts 15:14; 17:26, 27; Romans 11:5). . . . Finding the person of peace is the key to starting a house Ekklesia in any locality. He is easily identifiable because he is generally a person of good reputation and hospitable.

— VICTOR CHOUDHRIE, *The Church in Your House*

I (FELICITY) WAS watching a couple of squirrels chasing each other along the branches of the oak trees outside my bedroom window when I heard the words:

"You are to prayer-walk Oltorf."

Where did that come from? I wondered. The words seemed to come out of nowhere during my regular morning time with the Lord. Actually, experience has taught me that a thought from "left field" is one of the ways Jesus most commonly speaks to me.

It was probably a couple of months before I finally got around to walking Oltorf, a street about twenty minutes from our home. On my second day of walking, I came across a low-income housing project called Springfield. A large sign posted at the entrance warned that loitering was forbidden and everyone on the property must carry ID. As I wandered between the run-down row houses, past the Dumpsters and the abandoned cars, praying for the people who lived there, the Lord quietly whispered in my heart.

"You are to start a church here."

On the way back to the car, I met one of the neighbors of the complex and we started chatting.

"Do you see that hole?" he said, pointing to a small hole in the fence. "That's a bullet hole from a drive-by shooting. And that car," he continued, waving his arm in the direction of a flashy sedan that was driving past, "belongs to one of the drug dealers at Springfield."

Back in our simple church that weekend, I shared what I sensed the Lord wanted to be done. Others committed themselves to pray with me for the people who lived at Springfield. Occasionally we got together to pray, and once or twice we actually prayer-walked through the housing complex. But for the most part we prayed on our own.

About six months later, my husband, Tony, and I were driving along Oltorf.

"Why don't we prayer-walk Springfield? We have some spare time this morning."

We parked some distance away and made our way into the housing complex. What I did not realize was that Tony was specifically praying that we would meet our "person of peace" that day.

All of a sudden, the skies darkened and there was a torrential downpour. We dashed for the closest shelter, under a balcony where two middle-aged Hispanic women sat chatting in lawn chairs. We all commented on the weather, and then one of the women asked, "Why are you here?" It was obvious we weren't from around there.

"We're here to pray for your neighborhood," we told the women.

Over the next half hour we learned a little about Rosa and her sister, Alba. They were born into a Catholic family and vowed to die Catholic. Yet, because of an incident in their past, neither of them had darkened the door of a Catholic church for years. However, they knew God was real. Rosa told a remarkable story about one of her children

> "We're here to pray for your neighborhood," we told the women.

becoming seriously ill when he was very young. He experienced an angelic encounter and a dramatic healing.

As the rain slowed to a drizzle, Tony asked, "Would it be okay if we came by from time to time to pray about some of the needs in your family?"

Connecting with them was that simple. A couple of times a week we went to Rosa's house and prayed. We didn't stay long, just fifteen to twenty minutes. And God began to answer prayer. For two years, Rosa had been trying to get welfare checks; a couple of weeks after we prayed, the first check showed up. As our friendship with Rosa grew, we learned more about her family and some of the pressures they faced living in the projects.

About six weeks later, we asked Rosa if she wanted to invite other members of her family to hear about Jesus too. She liked the idea.

That same week Rosa introduced us to a lady who lived a few doors down from her.

"You'll like Angela," she told us. "She's like you."

Angela was a radiant, on-fire Christian who had been delivered from years of drug addiction when she accepted Christ. But that wasn't the only miracle that had happened to her—that very week she had gone from HIV positive to HIV negative following prayers for healing from members of her church. Angela's apartment reflected her great faith in God; it was orderly, and quiet worship music played in the background.

"This would be a great environment for Rosa's family,"

we thought. So we agreed that for our first meeting with Rosa's family, we would go to Angela's apartment instead of Rosa's.

What a disaster! None of Rosa's family showed up. We could also see how uncomfortable Rosa was with this group. Angela's church believed in using only the King James Version of the Bible. All the time we had been getting together with Rosa we had been using an easy-to-read version of the Bible. But because Angela insisted on using the KJV for the Bible study, it was too difficult for Rosa to understand. We could see that she was struggling.

When we got back home, we were discouraged. "Where did we go wrong, Lord?" we asked.

Then we remembered Luke 10:7, where it specifically says to stay in the home of the person of peace and not move from house to house.

"Lord, we're so sorry," we prayed. "We've messed up. Please get us out of this one!"

Watching God's Plan Unfold

A few days later, Angela received word that her request for an apartment outside of the projects had been granted. (She had been praying to move for months.) The following week, we were back at Rosa's house; it was chaotic but filled with love. Rosa has a heart the size of Texas—even strangers are family to her because of her amazing capacity to love people.

And her actual family members started coming. Rosa was

the first one to give her heart to the Lord. She prayed simply, as we shared with her in her living room. Her life was so transformed that other family members saw the difference. Two of her sisters became followers of Christ, then a couple of Rosa's kids, various nephews, nieces, grandkids, and other family members soon after. Other families from Springfield started coming. At one point, thirty-five people were crammed into Rosa's tiny apartment, sitting on the floor, on the stairs, and in the kitchen. Eventually Rosa's group spawned two other groups that met in other projects (although for various reasons, they eventually disbanded).

In Springfield, lives were transformed before our eyes. Rosa's youngest son, James, a talented eighteen-year-old rapper, was one of them.

Shortly after we started meeting at Rosa's, James made it clear why he could never become a Christian. Ever since he was a kid, a group of friends had been there for him; he knew that if he had to choose between his friends and Jesus, he would have to choose his friends. The following week a friend of ours named Norman, whom God often uses to speak to people about their situations,[1] came to the meeting.

> If James had to choose between his friends and Jesus, he would choose his friends.

"James, Jesus loves the fact that you are such a good friend," Norman told him.

Soon after that meeting, James went in for an appointment to give blood. The lab discovered some abnormalities in his blood during the routine screening process and advised James to see a doctor. Of course, James feared the worst. So he told the Lord, "If You will spare my life, You are going to be the One who has my honor and my respect from this day on!"

The problem with James's blood turned out to be minor, but the young rapper kept his word to the Lord. "Lord, from this day on, You are the One who has all my honor and my respect." Not only that, but over the next few days, he contacted all his friends and told them, "From this day on, my honor and respect belong to Jesus. If I ever have to choose between you and Jesus, I will choose Him!"

Group Dynamics

Each time we got together, we started with a meal; at times, it resembled a stampede to the table. On one particular occasion, we had barely finished the meal when a fight broke out between two of the kids. James took the troublemaker upstairs; he wanted the instigator to know how that kind of behavior in the projects around the wrong person could possibly get him shot. Then Rosa got involved, telling James that he was handling the situation all wrong. (This is church!) When things had settled down and the kids were outside, James posed a question to the rest of us.

"How do you handle it when you hate someone?"

For forty minutes, we discussed how a Christian should handle hatred, how to discipline kids, and what to do when Christians disagree. We read Bible passages, shared personal experiences, and prayed for each other. Then the kids joined us for a time of praise. At one point I looked up, and two kids about nine and eleven years old were singing their hearts out with their eyes closed. It may not have been the most in-tune worship, and it was certainly loud. But I thought to myself, *Jesus, You're here, and You love this!*

We experienced many supernatural answers to prayer at Rosa's house. That became a problem for us. Things were so exciting that we didn't want to leave this house church. But we knew it was important that the group be led by people from the projects. Eventually, when all the outsiders pulled out, Rosa was devastated.

"I feel like you don't love me anymore," she confessed.

It took quite a while for the group to recover, but James took over leadership and the different family members continue to grow. Life in the projects is never without problems and these have not been solved overnight, but now they have the presence of Jesus to help them.

Luke 10 Principles

All over the world, the Lord is using Luke 10:1-9 as a pattern for making disciples and gathering them together as churches. The principles found in this passage play a key part in all the major church-planting movements happening today, with thousands of churches being planted each week. But God isn't just working overseas. The story of Rosa and Springfield directly parallels Luke 10. Let's take a closer look.

- Verse 1: Jesus sends out seventy-two disciples, two by two, to all the towns and places where He planned to go. Jesus obviously had a master plan for reaching the region and He sent the disciples to specific locations. They weren't going out individually or in larger teams and Jesus was going to follow close behind. That's how the Lord led us to Springfield. Jesus has a strategy for your region too; your part is to listen to Jesus and do what He says.

- Verse 2: Jesus tells the disciples that the harvest is great but the laborers are few. He points out that the harvest is ready but He needs people to gather it in. As illustrated in Kenny's story in chapter 3, God honors prayers for laborers.

Prayer is the key to seeing God act. If we want to see God move by multiplying simple or organic churches, it takes intense prayer work on our parts. We are deceiving ourselves if we think it will just happen! We need to pray the price. In this verse, the disciples prayed for workers to come forward in the places they were going to visit. The laborers God uses are those who live among those who need to hear about Him. They are probably not even believers yet. This is a huge paradigm shift for the average Christian.

Prayer is the key to seeing God act.

Prayer walking has been a key strategy for church planting movements worldwide. As people go out in pairs to bless the area and its people, repent for the sins going on, bind the enemy, Satan, and pray for the welfare of the people who live there, an openness to the Gospel is created. A young couple in India tried an experiment. They picked two villages, and prayer-walked in only one of them. In the village where they prayer-walked, forty-five families became believers. They were thrown out of the other village.

- Verse 3: Jesus tells the disciples to go. The New Testament church was a "going" church, instead of a church that asked people to "come."

- Verse 4: The disciples are told not to take anything with them because they'd find material resources in the harvest for the short time they'd be there making disciples and training leaders. Leaders are to come from the harvest too. When we did not quickly hand over leadership to someone from the complex, we bred an unhealthy dependence on outsiders, which nearly shipwrecked the whole church. (Praise God, He covers our mistakes!) In rapidly multiplying church-planting movements, leadership is handed over quickly—within a matter of days to weeks—while the new leader is closely mentored by a more mature Christian—usually the person who led them to Christ.

> *A person of peace is someone who has a circle of influence and gives access to those people.*

- Verses 5 and 6: We are looking for a person who will invite us into his or her home. This is likely to be our "person of peace." A person of peace is someone who has a circle of influence and gives access to those people. Rosa was our person of peace at Springfield, first connecting us with her family, then others in her complex. The person of peace is often a person of reputation, whether good or bad. Lydia, an accomplished businesswoman in Acts 16, was a person of peace. But so was the woman at the well, whose reputation was not so savory (John 4). As that person gathers his or her friends, the discipleship process begins and this group is likely to be the foundation of any new church.

- Verse 7: We stay in that house, eating and drinking what is set before us. What is the reason for sharing food? To create relationships and enter into that person's culture. This may not be a comfortable process but if we turn down the food, we are rejecting more than the meal. This verse also tells us that we should not go from house to house. (What does that say about door-to-door evangelism?)

- Verse 8: Eating again! Do you see the importance of this? At this point, there is still no preaching or any other direct evangelism. We are continuing to build relationships.

- Verse 9: We are to heal the sick, expecting the Lord to intervene in their lives supernaturally. Only then do we have the right to speak to them about the Kingdom of God. Once they have watched the Lord work, they will be open. When Rosa's welfare checks started coming within two weeks of praying for her, the door was unlocked for us at Springfield. It is more effective to start making disciples in the home of the person of peace with his friends and family than to invite the person of peace to come to our church.

If we ask God for opportunities to pray for people's needs, He will give them to us. It is risky business to step out in faith and offer to pray for someone. But God delights in answering that kind of prayer.

7

THE HOLY SPIRIT LEADS US

The Man Who Followed God's Directions

For all who are led by the Spirit of God are children of God.
— ROMANS 8:14

☼ To live a God-centered life, you must focus your life on God's purposes, not your own plans. You must seek to see from God's perspective rather than from your own distorted human perspective. When God starts to do something in the world, He takes the initiative to come and talk to somebody. For some divine reason, He has chosen to involve His people in accomplishing His purposes.

— HENRY T. BLACKABY AND CLAUDE V. KING,
Experiencing God

FRANK AND HIS wife, Betty, have been married for more than fifty-six years, but things haven't always gone smoothly for them. At one point in their marriage, Frank and Betty separated, and during that time Frank sensed the Lord leading him to move from the West Coast to a city in the Midwest. He had always wanted to live in the inner city and this was his opportunity. So Frank bought an old house for zero money down and rented out rooms to cover part of the house payments.

For some years before moving to the Midwest, Frank was the consulting chaplain at a drug and alcohol rehab center in Southern California. He worked with prisoners, addicts, and homeless people and became convinced that from that group he could find potential church leaders. When Frank moved he handpicked some of the men from the rehab center whom he felt were called by God for ministry. They lived with Frank and were trained for outreach.

Prior to moving to the Midwest, Frank made a trip there to look for a house. A friend, Bob, lived there and was going to help him. As Frank prayed in preparation for the trip, he saw a face in his mind.

Who can this be? he thought to himself. *I don't recognize him.*

The face Frank pictured was distinctive. The man looked Italian, with dark hair drawn back from his face and a mustache.

A few days later, on the long drive from California, Frank could sense God speaking to him, directing him to go to the corner of Crockett and Carthage when he arrived at his destination. Frank knew that the person he had "seen" while praying would be in a restaurant near that intersection. When Frank arrived in the city and picked up Bob, they headed to that location.

It was a bad part of town. The houses were run-down and abandoned cars seemed to be everywhere.

"There must be a restaurant here somewhere," Frank said.

Nothing even resembled a restaurant. Then Frank noticed a dark building with a dim light over the door. He could barely make out the faded sign on the door: Bar Open. It was a cheerless-looking place.

> **Frank knew that the person he had "seen" while praying would be in a specific restaurant.**

"There's no way I'm going into that dive," Bob said. "I'll stay in the car."

Frank parked the car, got out, and locked the doors behind him. Picking his way through the trash on the sidewalk, he made his way to the door and opened it. It was pitch black inside and the room reeked of decay, smoke, and stale beer. As his eyes adjusted, Frank could see a bar in front of him. A couple of men sitting on bar stools gazed into the distance with vacant expressions, only turning to look when Frank walked in. Frank got the impression that no one there liked strangers.

In a lounge area behind the bar, the ceiling tiles were coming down. Frank approached a woman there who was clearing dirty glasses and emptying ashtrays.

"Is there a restaurant near here?" he asked.

"I'm just about done here," she said, identifying herself as the bar owner. "There's a café a couple of blocks away. If you follow me in your car, I'll take you there."

As she finished wiping down the tables with a dirty cloth, the woman asked Frank what brought him to the city. "God is leading me to live here," he answered.

Frank and his friend followed the woman a few blocks and saw a dilapidated-looking storefront with a sign in the window: Bistro and Eatery. But because it was late, Frank decided to come back the next day.

The next morning Frank drove back to the restaurant by himself. It looked even more ramshackle in the daylight. He pushed open the dirty glass door and there, through an archway, he saw a person sitting at a table.

It's him! Frank realized with astonishment. *It's the man I pictured!*

> **Frank stopped. The man was wearing a dress!**

Frank walked between the tables covered with red-checked plastic cloths, making his way toward the man. But as he rounded the corner, he stopped. The man was wearing a dress!

In fact, it wasn't a man at all. It was a woman who was slightly balding, with dark hair combed straight back and dark facial hair. (The mustache was real.) Frank was astonished.

"When I was praying the other day, I saw you," Frank said. "Can I talk to you?"

He sat down opposite her. As they talked, Frank learned that the woman's name was Nora. Half Native American and half black, she had been ostracized by both groups. Many people would consider her a throwaway; she was badly damaged in many ways. Although she was only in her fifties, she looked much older. Her husband, who washed dishes in the restaurant, was a full-blown alcoholic. Nora told Frank that she had tried different churches but felt rejected in each one. Although she wanted to believe in God, she didn't believe He heard her prayers.

"I'd like to come to your house to talk with you and your husband about how Jesus can be more involved in your lives," Frank said. Nora was open to the idea and took him there to meet some of her grandchildren. Later that evening, Frank returned to hold a meeting for Nora, her husband, and the grandchildren.

Frank and Nora met several times and though they eventually stopped meeting in her home, Frank knows that the Lord is moving in her life. But even more important, Frank has learned that following the promptings of the Holy Spirit can be an adventure.

Fitting into the Neighborhood

Remember the house that Frank bought? Three or four men striving to follow Jesus lived there with him. All of the men came out of various addictions and problems but now were sober and leading productive lives. That house became the center of a new church and a place where God began doing His work.

The Christians decided to bring the neighbors together to celebrate community members' birthdays. People from the neighborhood wouldn't come to a regular simple church meeting, but everyone loved birthday parties. After the meal and birthday cake, the men prayed for and blessed the person who was marking another year. Often the Lord directed and spoke to the birthday person clearly and wonderful things happened to them. As a result, more and more people wanted to get involved.

Andy had been one of the California rehab center residents whom Frank had befriended. After surrendering his life to Jesus, Andy went to Bible school before joining Frank in the Midwest. When Frank and Betty reunited and he returned to California, Andy stayed with the men in the house and became the leader of the work there. Young people from the community were drawn to Andy because he spent a lot of time with them. They played baseball and hung out together in the park. Andy had a pit bull—the dog of choice in their neighborhood—that helped him reach out to others, especially other dog owners.

> People wouldn't come to a regular simple church meeting, but everyone loved birthday parties.

Back in California Frank was thrilled to hear that several of the young people from the Midwest house had become Christians under Andy's leadership. A couple of teenagers were baptized in a swimming pool and others in a kids' wading pool in the basement of the house. Seven or eight people, none of whom had known Christ previously, regularly got together on Sundays. They experienced exponential spiritual growth. A couple in their sixties whom Frank never expected to embrace Jesus committed their lives to the Lord. The wife, who had been illiterate, began learning to read so she could study her Bible.

When the church members got together, it tended to be nonreligious and unstructured but full of life. They shared a meal together each week and talked about things going on in their lives. They prayed for one another and cared for one another. Nobody put on a phony front. People were real with each other and appreciated what God was doing in their lives.

Frank's vision for training leaders from tough backgrounds came to pass; the new church was a great training ground for them. Andy has since moved back to California and the other members of the Midwest church have gone their various ways. But what they experienced together strongly illustrates how God loves to lead His people—like Frank—to a ripe harvest field.

Following Where the Holy Spirit Leads

House church planter Wolfgang Simson[1] likes to say that programs are what the church is reduced to when the Holy Spirit leaves!

Jesus was able to say He did only what He saw the Father do and spoke only what He learned from the Father (John 5:19-20; 8:28). The same can be true for us.

How do we know what God is doing? Here's an example: Someone mentions a problem to you and you ask, "Have you ever thought of praying about this situa-tion?" The person replies, "I feel like my prayers are just hitting the ceiling." This is an open door to a spiritual con-versation, evidence of God at work.

In Luke 10:1-9, Jesus told the disciples where they were to go. We need to hear Jesus tell us where He wants us to make disciples and where He plans to build His church. Which subculture should we be working with? Which apart-ment complex should we pray for on a regular basis?

Hearing the voice of God is a skill that can be learned. In John 10:4 (NASB), Jesus says, "The sheep follow him [the shepherd] because they know his voice." The way to know Jesus' voice is to spend time with Him. If I were in a room of fifty people who were all talking, I still would instantly distinguish the voice of my husband, Tony. I have spent so much time with him that I recognize his voice. The same is true with Jesus. Obviously, anything we hear from God is to be measured against the plumb line of Scripture.

Many years ago when I was doing a considerable amount of counseling, I spent time waiting on the Lord before I met with the person who needed help. I prayed for the person and then I wrote what I sensed the Lord was saying to me about his or her situation (the thoughts came spontaneously to my mind). After I had spent time with the person, I went back to my notes to see if what I thought the Lord had said to me was relevant to that person's situation. Remarkably, 85 to 90 percent of the time it was. Over the years, I have learned to hear Jesus' voice. For me, the voice of Jesus often comes through a thought (or a picture in my mind) that seems to come out of nowhere!

Once after a church meeting, a young girl who was depressed asked me to help her. As we walked to a secluded corner, I asked the Lord what her problem was. I had a quick impression that she may have been sexually abused by her father when she was a child. It took two questions to arrive at the root of her problem: "Tell me about your relationship with your father"; "Did he abuse you in any way?" (Notice that I did not say, "The Lord told me you were sexually abused by your father." It is embarrassing if you get it wrong, and it also gives the person an easy way out if he or she doesn't want to admit the truth of what you are saying.)

> *Many people never follow Jesus because church is a big stumbling block for them.*

We not only hear God speaking to us through the Word or through listening to His voice in our hearts; we can also hear Him through each other. Increasingly, God is leading people to listen to Him corporately, often over several days. We must lay down our own agendas and seek His Kingdom's purposes together. At times God chooses to reveal something to a group of people, rather than individuals—something they have both the ability and authority to respond to together. We (together) can have the mind of Christ (1 Corinthians 2:16).

As Frank's story shows, many people never follow Jesus because church is a big stumbling block for them. It was what Mahatma Gandhi was intimating when he said, "I like your Christ; I do not like your Christians. Your Christians are so unlike your Christ." But in the book of Acts, we see the opposite. There was something very winsome about the believers in the New Testament church (Acts 2:47; 5:13-14).

For many of us, our Christian walk is based on performance, on obligation and duty—we try to earn God's approval yet often feel like we fail. (*If only I prayed more, evangelized more . . .*) Sadly, guilt and shame become our motivation for trying to live a life pleasing to Him.

For far too many Christians, life is a rule book of "dos and don'ts"—especially the don'ts! Jesus didn't die to give us a set of rules. He died that we might have life—abundantly (John 10:10). Ezekiel 36:26 describes the new covenant relationship that happens when we become disciples of Jesus: "And I will give you a new heart, and I will put a new spirit in you. I will take out your stony, stubborn heart and give you a tender, responsive heart."

When we become Christians, God gives us new natures—hearts with His laws already written on them (Hebrews 8:10). If we are walking close to Jesus, His grace and love working within us motivate us to *want* to do what legalistic Christianity says we *ought* to do. The outcome may look the same, but the inner motivation is profoundly different. And other people sense the difference.

If we give nonbelievers the impression that the Christian life is restrictive, that God is waiting to pounce on us if we color outside the lines, why would they want to join us? But if they see that we experience joy and peace even when things are going wrong, they want to know more. The joy-filled and vibrant walk of someone living in close relationship with Jesus is contagious.

8

GOOD SOIL

The Man Who Believed God Could Never Love Him

The seed that fell on good soil represents those who truly hear and understand God's word and produce a harvest of thirty, sixty, or even a hundred times as much as had been planted! — MATTHEW 13:23

☼ I have always been amazed at what can happen when we simply plant the good seed of God's Word in the good soil of broken people. We have an expression in our movement: bad people make good soil—there's a lot of fertilizer in their lives.

— NEIL COLE, *Organic Church*

FROM THE VERY beginning, life was tough for Sam. When he was four years old, Sam contracted scarlet fever. He was isolated from the rest of the family because they feared infection. The only human contact he had for weeks was with an aunt, who looked after him a couple of hours each day. Sam's older sister pushed his food into the room on a wheeled tray. Neither of his parents went near Sam.

When Sam overheard the doctor tell his aunt one day, "It's unlikely he's going to make it through the night," the young boy thought he must have done something really bad for God to let this happen to him.

But Sam did recover and not long afterward the family moved to California. By the time Sam was in school, he had started acting up and his father had started beating him. But after every beating, he told Sam, "I'm only doing this because I love you." That type of "love" only confused Sam more.

After being punished, Sam would crawl into the sewer pipe behind his house. There he begged and prayed, "God, will You please stop my dad from loving me!"

When Sam was twelve, he prepared for his first Holy Communion in the Catholic church. The nuns had taught Sam that if he took the bread and wine in an unworthy manner, he could get sick or die. Sam knew that if he didn't take Communion, his dad would be humiliated and Sam would get a beating. At the altar, just as the priest was about to put the bread onto his tongue, Sam fainted. Afterward, his sister said, "I thought God struck you dead because you're so bad!" Sam's sense that God was rejecting him grew deeper.

A few years later his parents divorced. Sam's anger became even more explosive, his sisters often receiving the brunt of his pent-up emotions. One day when his older sister threw herself across his younger sister to protect her from his rage, Sam saw what he had become.

"I will never touch another person in anger," he vowed.

Sam's mom soon remarried. His new stepfather didn't hit Sam, but he yelled at him constantly. When Sam turned sixteen, his mother asked him to leave home. Sam lived with his dad less than a year before joining the navy.

He used to hitchhike from the base in San Diego to Los Angeles. One day, a man picked him up—a friend of a friend. The man drugged and raped Sam. When Sam got back to the base later that day, he found a letter from his mom saying that she had disowned him as her son. Something in Sam died then.

A Turning Point

When Sam was eighteen, he married a beautiful Mexican girl named Gloria from Texas. He was still in the navy but he was drinking heavily and using drugs—LSD, speed, and marijuana mixed with elephant tranquilizers (PCP). A year and a half later, he was discharged.

Gloria's family considered Sam an outsider because he wasn't Mexican. One night her brothers and cousins confronted Sam. They wanted to start a gang, and turned on Sam. His brother-in-law threw a chair at Sam and it hit his left eye, causing it to swell immediately.

Sam and Gloria ran for their car and sped off, not realizing that the others were following. When the couple got home, their pursuers blocked the driveway with their car. The men pulled Sam from the car, while his wife ran into the house to call the police. Three of his attackers held Sam down while the fourth went looking for a pipe to beat him. The only thing that Sam could see was a church bus parked in a neighbor's driveway.

At that moment God seemed to say to him, "Up until now, you've run your life your way. Why not try doing it My way?"

Somehow those words gave Sam the strength to get away. When the police arrived, he did not press charges because his wife begged him not to.

But in that brief moment, God had come into Sam's life. From that point on, he knew Jesus as his Savior. However, he assumed that living a holy life was following a rule book of dos and don'ts. For six years, Sam tried to obey what his church taught was real Christianity, but he couldn't do it. The church was controlling every detail of its members' lives. As time went on, Sam could see how this control was damaging his family. He finally went to see his pastor.

> "You've run your life your way. Why not try doing it My way?" God seemed to say.

"My wife and I are considering leaving the church," he told him. "We feel that God is leading us elsewhere."

The pastor looked at him sternly, then pronounced, "You

will never amount to anything in life because you're leaving my umbrella of protection." Sam was determined to prove the pastor wrong.

Resolved that his life would amount to something and he would be successful at whatever he did, Sam moved into the business world. He became involved politically and developed a number of programs in hospitals. Well known and respected among his peers and superiors, Sam became facility director of a hospital. With an impressive office and a salary to match, he felt that life was good. However, his family life was going downhill fast.

Late one night, Sam was awakened by a phone call from the hospital. "You'd better get down here. Your son Ben has been shot. He's in critical condition and we're not sure he's going to make it."

Sam's sixteen-year-old son, Ben, was in a gang and had been shot by a rival gang member. His heart actually stopped twice in the ambulance on the way to the hospital and once in the emergency room. Every time, God brought him back. After two surgeries and three weeks in the hospital, Ben fully recovered.

But the gang members who had shot Ben wouldn't leave his family alone. Sam tried to act like life was normal, but he had an overwhelming fear that the gang would make an attempt on his family's lives.

So Sam sent the family out of state to stay with one of Gloria's cousins, while he remained behind, making final preparations to leave his job. He sent money to the family for the next two months. But when he joined them, he learned that Gloria's cousin had taken all the money for himself. Sam got into a fight with the relative and the family was thrown out on the street in the worst snowstorm in decades.

The family ended up in a Salvation Army family safe center, where they lived for two months until Sam found a job. He managed a crew that set up modular office spaces. He climbed the corporate ladder again, but inside his heart felt numb.

As things in his family continued to deteriorate, Sam assumed that God was angry with him but he didn't care. Now thirty-eight, Sam had sex with a twelve-year-old girl he befriended. The reality of what he had done jolted Sam to his senses.

Coming Clean

Sam finally saw himself for who he was. He was so ashamed that he left his family. Twice he attempted to take his own life—first by crashing his car, then by jumping off a cliff onto the rocky shore of a river. In the second attempt, he landed in the river and its current pulled him away from the rocks. Sam was angry with God for not letting him die.

He arrived at the Union Gospel Mission soaking wet. After he had been there for a couple of days, the man in charge of the dayroom invited Sam to his office.

"What brought you to the mission, Sam?" he asked.

Without thinking, Sam confessed everything he had done. "I wanted that man at the mission to hate me. It would have given me strength to go out and finish taking my life," he later admitted. But after hearing Sam's confession, the man said, "Sam, a month ago I would have called you scum. But today I know God's love differently, and I welcome you as my brother!" He walked over to Sam and gave him a hug.

Sam's life changed completely that day. For the first time in his life, he experienced real love—unconditionally. As he met other people at the mission who showed God's love to him, Sam was ready to call out to God Himself.

"God, if You will clean up my life inside and outside, I will go anywhere and do anything. But You have to do the work. I've already proven I can't."

When Sam got up from his knees, he felt clean. But he knew that the first thing he needed to do was to turn himself in to the police for having sex with a minor. "I want to turn myself in. I've committed a crime that you need to know about. Is there a detective I can talk to?" he asked the desk clerk on the phone. Sam was instructed to come to the station and meet with the detectives. Since the crime had not been reported to the police, they just let Sam talk.

"You've done a good thing in confessing, Sam," said the detectives. "We're going to investigate to make sure it's all true. However, since you brought this information forward yourself, we're going to release you on your own recognizance. We don't see you as a threat or a flight risk."

Sam was later booked and released until his trial. He stayed at the mission, receiving pastoral help and encouragement.

At the trial, Sam was found guilty and was sentenced to seventy-eight months in prison.

Life in Prison

Sam was scared in prison—so scared he thought he might die from fear. The fear was so thick that it actually had a smell. But God began to show Sam that He would protect and use him there.

Sam's cell became a meeting place where men could come and pour out their hearts. Many of them received the Lord, meeting from cell to cell—it was literally a "cell church"! Up and down the tiers, little groups met. They broke bread together using cherry Kool-Aid and crackers. The official church inside the prison grew. In a prison population of 1,500, the church grew from six to a hundred and fifty by the time Sam left six years later.

> **Whenever they heard a riot was being organized, Jim and Sam prayed. Three prison riots were stopped by prayer.**

Jim became one of Sam's closest brothers in Christ. Whenever they heard a riot was being organized, they sat in the middle of the prison yard and prayed. Three prison riots were stopped by prayer.

Another time, Jim grabbed Sam and they headed to the chapel. (Jim and Sam had received permission to go to the chapel an hour before each service to set up chairs and pray over the building.)

As soon as they walked into the chapel, Jim dropped to

his knees and started crying out to God. "Lord, cleanse this house! We repent for what has gone on here. Please come and cleanse this house." The two men prayed over everything—the doors, the chairs, the altar, the music equipment.

Two weeks later, the prison chaplain came up to them with a puzzled look on his face. "Do you know what's just happened?" he asked.

"No. What?"

"The Wiccans and the Native Americans who practice their tribal religions just visited me. They said I need to get them a different building to meet in. When I asked them why, they said, 'There's something wrong in this place. . . . We can't raise our spirits here anymore!'"

When Sam was released from prison, he went back to the mission, completing a two-year discipleship program. But church life outside the prison was frustrating for Sam. The people weren't as open and real as his Christian brothers in prison. God seemed dead to people on the outside; they only talked about what God did six or ten years ago, not what He was doing today.

Why aren't these people experiencing God now? Sam asked himself. Many days, Sam found himself wanting to go back to prison—God was real there.

Sweet Gospel

Sam knew he had to do something or he would end up back in prison. So he and a couple of other Christians started an outreach at a local restaurant. They called it SCUM—Simple Christians Under Maintenance.

One day a friend named Jenny asked Sam if he would go with her to a cemetery where her uncle was buried. While Jenny placed flowers on her uncle's grave, Sam scouted out the surrounding area. SCUM had outgrown the restaurant and they were looking for a new place to meet. Sam and Jenny spotted a large grassy area down the hill from the cemetery.

"This would be perfect for a SCUM outreach," Jenny commented. As they looked around them, they noticed some makeshift huts and a couple under a blanket.

"Oh, no! This is People's Park," exclaimed Jenny. People's Park is a nudist colony where anything goes. Some sections are peaceful, but drugs, sex, homosexuality, and witchcraft run rampant in other areas. People had even been murdered there.

Sam and Jenny left as quickly as they could. But when they got to the car, they both spontaneously started weeping, realizing that they had judged the people living there.

"What can we do that would make a difference here?" Jenny said.

They decided to make "friendship candy bars." Sam wrote poems that Jenny illustrated and they wrote Scripture verses on labels, taping them to Hershey's candy bars. He and Jenny took a bucket of the candy bars down to People's Park with some ice and some more poems in plastic sleeves.

As they left, they prayed and claimed the area for Jesus Christ.

About a month later, Sam was sitting at a table in a restaurant, writing, when a young man approached him.

"You look like a Christian. Can I talk to you?" he asked.

Sam wondered what made him look like a Christian. He didn't have a Bible on the table and he wasn't wearing a T-shirt with a Christian saying.

"Sure, sit down. You look hungry. Let me get you something to eat."

Jeff started telling his story. "My parents are ministers, and all my life they have talked to me about Jesus. They would get frustrated with me because I wouldn't accept Christianity. The other night I couldn't sleep so I went out walking. I walked for several hours, and I kept telling God, 'If You are really there like my parents say You are, and if You really love me the way they say You do, I need a miracle!' On my way back—you're not going to believe this—I found this bucket filled with candy bars with labels on them talking about friendship with God and how much He loves me."

Sam prayed with Jeff to receive the Lord that day. Three weeks later, Sam was once again in the restaurant when Jeff came in with several of his friends.

"No way! This is the dude I was telling you about!" Jeff exclaimed to his friends. They all crowded into the booth with him.

"What's that?" Jeff asked, looking at the book of poems Sam had open on the table. He looked at the book, then he looked at Sam. It suddenly hit him.

"No way! That was you?" He started crying and told his

friends, "This is the dude who wrote that stuff on the candy bars!" His friends were so amazed that all but one of them received the Lord that day.

Redeeming Felony Flats

Eventually Sam moved from the mission into an apartment located in a drug-infested neighborhood. Sam, Jenny, and a couple of other Christians started a Bible study at his apartment with people from the streets. Initially, seven people came; then twelve, twenty, forty-five. Sam moved the meeting outside. The next night, ninety-plus people filled the front yard! God worked in miraculous ways—food was multiplied, people were healed, and many received Christ and were set free.

Sam and Jenny called the group "Off Broadway"—partly because the apartment was on a street called Broadway, and partly because they helped people off the broad way and onto the narrow way with Jesus.

It wasn't long before Sam's work got the attention of influential pastors in the area. They asked Sam to be the prayer coordinator for his section of the city.

He replied, "I have no training except for what I learned in prison. I was tested and challenged there on everything I believe. I have no degrees. I know what it's like to walk in darkness, and I believe God wants to use me to help people make the transition into His Kingdom of light."

For a few short moments, you could have heard a pin

drop. Then one man stood up. "Sam, I wish we had a hundred more men just like you!"

The group of pastors rose to their feet, surrounded Sam, and laid hands on him. As they anointed him with oil, they said, "Go! You are doing what God has called you to do!"

The whole neighborhood changed during the time Sam lived in the apartment. Within a year, all the drug houses moved from the neighborhood. Still, Sam was a little disappointed. He didn't want them to relocate; he wanted them to change!

Sam moved to another apartment in an area known as Felony Flats, and he wasted no time getting to know his neighbors. Once again God moved, and soon Sam was sharing Christ with more than two hundred people in the front yard of the building.

> "I know what it's like to walk in darkness. I believe God wants me to help people into His Kingdom of light."

When Sam moved into his new neighborhood, there were five major drug houses on the street connected to three drug cartels. Now only one drug house is there, and it is not part of any cartel. Although one drug house relocated, the others have not. Instead, they have changed! God answered Sam's prayer.

For more than twenty years, people from different churches have prayer-walked these streets. Sam is convinced that what he is seeing happen is a result of their collective prayers. They planted and watered, and now it is harvesttime!

God's Amazing Grace

One evening, one of the people who regularly prayer-walks called Sam. "I want to get a group together to pray over the drug house just around the corner from you," he said.

Sam and his friends agreed to get together with him around 10:00 p.m., when activity picked up around the house. As people entered and left the drug house, they had to pass through the group of praying believers who were standing six feet from the door. Sam could tell that the "customers" didn't know how to react to them; they looked visibly shaken!

All of a sudden, the Holy Spirit moved the group of Christians to sing. "Amazing grace! how sweet the sound that saved a wretch like me! . . ."

The sweet melody wafted through the evening air. Soon the lights in the drug house were turned off—business was shut down for the night. The Christians returned home.

The next day, Sam's friend who organized the prayer vigil returned to the drug house. The woman who ran it came out and began sharing her story.

Nancy was raised in the church; both her parents had been pastors. When they both died at an early age, Nancy blamed God for taking them and rebelled against Him.

"I'm stuck now. I don't have a choice. I'm in too far," Nancy said. "But you know, last night, when you guys started singing 'Amazing Grace,' I couldn't control myself. I cried and cried."

A few weeks later, there was a knock on Sam's door. Nancy

was standing there. "I wanted you to know I've left all that stuff," she said. "The drugs, the money, everything. And now I'm about to turn myself in! I'm not too worried about being locked up because I'm no longer locked up here," she said, pointing to her heart and smiling.

"Nancy, could I give you a hug?"

"I'd really like that."

"Keep in contact with us because we'll walk through this with you. Jesus loves you!"

Two hours after Nancy left Sam's house to turn herself in, the police raided her house with a warrant for her arrest.

The work of Off Broadway continues, although Sam has moved to another state. God has produced a great harvest from the "bad soil" Sam believed represented his life.

Good Soil

Jesus tells us that the fields are ripe and ready to harvest (John 4:35). Why aren't we seeing more fruit in the church today?

In the parable of the sower, Jesus describes four different kinds of soil—only one is good soil that produces a plentiful harvest (Matthew 13:3-23). What makes a person into good soil?

Jesus has been described as a "friend of sinners." He was renowned for hanging around tax collectors and sinners (Matthew 11:19)—eating, drinking, and attending their parties (Mark 2:15-17; Luke 5:27-32). He didn't flinch when a prostitute anointed His feet with perfume (Luke 7:36-50). But we are often so scared of being contaminated by sin that we won't go to the places where these people are found. Or we're concerned that someone will see us and get the wrong impression!

If we stay isolated in nice middle-class neighborhoods, we are not nearly as likely to see a bountiful harvest of souls as in places where people know they have a need. People who have problems are often more receptive to the gospel. How about going to an AA meeting with a friend who is struggling with alcoholism? Or working with homeless people or people just released from jail?

Jesus has been described as a "friend of sinners."

We are also more likely to reap a harvest if we go to places where people are seeking spiritual answers. For example, I recently heard of a group of Christians who offer "dream interpretation" at spiritual festivals for New Age followers. This provides them with a ready access to people who are looking for spirituality.

Sam and the people he works with are good soil. God is using them powerfully to reach many.

9

JESUS IS BUILDING HIS CHURCH

The Man Who Seized God's Opportunities

Speak the truth in love, growing in every way more and more like Christ, who is the head of his body, the church. He makes the whole body fit together perfectly. As each part does its own special work, it helps the other parts grow, so that the whole body is healthy and growing and full of love. — EPHESIANS 4:15-16

☸ For the true Christian the one supreme test for the present soundness and ultimate worth of everything religious must be the place our Lord occupies in it. Is He Lord or symbol? Is He in charge of the project or merely one of the crew? Does He decide things or only help to carry out the plans of others? All religious activities . . . may be proved by the answer to the question, Is Jesus Christ Lord in this act?

— A. W. TOZER, *The Waning Authority of Christ in the Churches*

"So, David, what do you think about tattoos?"

David, a maintenance supervisor for a jewelry manufac-
turer, was working in the plant alongside his two friends,
John and Harry. He turned and saw John pointing to his
upper arm. Since there was rarely a topic the three didn't
discuss, they often had lively conversations.

"Tattoos show who you belong to, where your identity is. I
belong to my heavenly Father and am marked with His name
on my heart. My identity comes from my Father through
Jesus Christ. I am a son of God. Who do you belong to?"

Over the next two hours, David learned things about
Harry and John he never knew before. Harry attended a
church, but really had no idea about the things David was
saying about Jesus; John, a committed member of the Church
of the Latter-Day Saints (LDS), had lots of questions.

"What if I came to your home and we studied the Bible
to find the answers to some of these questions?" David
suggested.

He began a simple church with four couples from work—
only two with any meaningful relationship with God—meeting at one of their homes. David explained that Jesus came
to earth to die for our sins, restoring our relationship with
God. Within a month or so, all of them had committed their
lives to the Lord.

A few weeks later, David overheard John chatting with a
woman (another LDS member) who worked next to him,
sharing some of the things he had been learning at his new
church. Knowing David was within earshot, John would fire

a question at him every so often to get help. At the end of the afternoon, the woman came up to David.

"I know I've been taught wrong. Please, will you teach me?" After this woman became a follower of Jesus, she joined with eight other women whom David had ministered to and they formed their own church.

At work, if any of the other employees have a need—health concerns, family concerns, or anything else—they know David will pray for them. (When David heads out to the garage with someone, everyone knows what it's for.)

Thirty-five people work with David at the company, and five simple churches have resulted from his work.

David's Spiritual Journey

David was raised in a Pentecostal church. After he left Bible school, he worked as an assistant pastor in a small, rural church. When the senior pastor asked him to lead a cell group ministry, David was horrified. He thought cell groups undermined the larger church body and often led to church splits. However, he soon realized that God had given him an ability to initiate cell groups. In his church of a hundred people, David started twenty-three cells. (Not all the people who were in the cells came to the main church meetings.)

David and his wife, Vickie, moved to their current small town at the request of their senior pastor. The pastor hoped David could begin new cell groups there. Despite David's best efforts, however, he couldn't get one cell group started.

The work collapsed, but David was convinced that he and his wife should stay where they were.

The two of them launched out on their own, though still under the auspices of the original church. When David became part of a local pastors' prayer group, God opened his eyes. His denomination thought they were right about everything and everyone else was wrong. David no longer believed that was true.

At the time, David was shepherding a small storefront church with about forty members. Over the next few months, several things changed David's understanding of church. First, a man named Robert Fitts came and spoke to the church about the scriptural basis of church in the home. Robert helps simple churches establish outreach ministries, such as ministry-training schools, healing-prayer clinics, "All about Jesus" retreats, and "Into His Presence" worship gatherings.[1] David was ready to apply some of what he heard, but certainly not all of it—it was much too radical!

> **A true apostle raises up people and releases them to build the Kingdom of God.**

Another local leader challenged David's group to learn to distinguish between true apostles and false apostles. A false apostle raises up people to build his own ministry. A true apostle raises up people and releases them to build the Kingdom of God.

David's friend, a Bible bookstore manager, gave him information written by Wolfgang Simson about house churches.

Simson is a church growth specialist who has written extensively on the house church movement. His book *Houses That Change the World* has been used all over the world as a guide for starting simple churches. Initially, David kept saying to his friend, "Stop it! What do I want with that stuff?" But then he began reading it and the idea of simple churches took root in his mind.

God Works Locally

In 2003, the Lord took away David's church building, and the group began meeting in homes. Originally they thought the Lord would provide another building. But now, with the addition of cell groups that David has started, their vision is not to be relegated to one building but instead to start more and more churches wherever they can.

One of the men in the church is a recovering alcoholic, set free from his addiction through God's power. He continues to go to weekly Alcoholics Anonymous meetings, where he tells people about Jesus. He leads them to pray to God, the true Higher Power.

Another group, started by a Native American woman, gathers on an Indian reservation. When she moved away, David began leading it.

One day as David was driving past a coffee shop, he felt compelled to stop and go inside. He discovered that the owners were Christians and they became friends. One of the cell groups now meets there on Saturday mornings. Six or seven of them get together and bring friends who are nonbelievers. Over coffee, they present Jesus Christ as the truth and the answer to life's questions.

Over a two-year period David's church has seen thirteen different groups form, meeting in homes or in coffee shops. Every day before work begins at the jewelry company, the believers get together for Bible study and prayer with the encouragement of their employer.

How is all this happening? Let's ask David.

"The Lord is making this thing happen at a grassroots level, person to person. We tell people that they are the seeds of the Kingdom, and wherever the wind of the Holy Spirit blows them is where they're supposed to be. We suggest to people that they pray for a chance to speak to one person about Jesus. Then they walk with an opportunity mind-set until the Lord opens a door. As soon as they see a door of opportunity open for a relationship, they walk through it. They are not trying to convert the person, but merely letting the Lord create a friendship. They soon find that they can talk to the friend about Jesus. Then they suggest that they read Scripture together. Others soon join them. That's how disciples are being made and churches are multiplying locally."

> People are the seeds of the Kingdom. Wherever the wind of the Holy Spirit blows them is where they're supposed to be.

Sometimes the churches come together for larger meetings. With no building to accommodate them, they use different parks around the city. Over the past two years, park meetings have become one of the main ways for the churches to connect—not just in the city, but regionally as well. The Lord brings someone into town with a message for the churches, and a meeting is organized around their visit— sometimes in just a few days. In the past two years, people have come from many other countries, as well as from the United States. During the winter, when it's far too cold to meet outdoors, friends from traditional churches allow them to use their buildings.

God Works Regionally

God is building His church not only at David's job or in his city. It's plain that He is also doing something remarkable on a regional basis. Through a series of relationships across an area of several hundred square miles from city to city, God is creating a network of friendships.

This is how David describes it:

"I have a vision of a net stretching across the region. The knots signify relationships. The net is designed to bring in the harvest. At the moment, the Lord is not drawing in the net because it would break. But as it grows stronger, He will start to use it.

"Sometimes when I meet someone, the Lord will put it into my heart that this is important, and I will take their name. And the Lord is building strategic relationships with some of those people.

"For example, near the original church where I was associate pastor many years ago, a church was going through renewal. I used to make fun of them and call them the 'Church of the Weird'! Then when I moved here, I met them. I confessed my attitude to them and repented with tears. Later, when we were visiting them in their small city, they introduced us to some people from another city. We fell in love with each other, out there in the middle of nowhere. Over the course of time, we have both started simple churches. They have three or four groups in their city.

"On another occasion someone called our home by mistake, and we found out about two simple churches we didn't know existed in a neighboring city. They were being led by dynamic leaders and were bursting out of their homes. We put them in touch with each other and helped them see that they needed to multiply. Now they work together and have joint meetings. They have groups full of spiritually mature people who could easily be doing what they do. We challenged them to encourage people to look for opportunities in their homes and on their jobs to start reproducing the family. Now they are sending people out to start new groups.

> **"We want to do what the New Testament church did and discover the reason why they did it."**

"God is putting together a network of people with similar regional vision. We are beginning to work together. We had a meeting recently with people from eight different cities separated by more than 450 miles.

"I believe the Lord is preparing this net for the final harvest. Wherever people end up, they need to land with their eyes wide open to see what God is doing and then join Him in it. We're looking to raise spiritual sons, who become fathers, who can, in turn, raise sons. We want to see the Kingdom reproduced through these family relationships. And we are finding that He is leading us to the right places and He is tying the knots.

"We're looking to be led by the Lord, not just follow a ritual or formula. We don't only want to do what we see in the New Testament. We want to see why they did what they did. We don't want to miss planting the seed that produces fruit. God is doing something unique in each area and we want to find it, not just follow someone else's pattern.

"God is orchestrating a collection of relationships. We didn't sit down and try to figure it out. We are watching the Lord do something dynamic and special, created in His mind, not ours. Jesus is building His church!"

Ongoing Construction

Church is not about buildings or meetings; it's not about church structure or charismatic leaders. Church is about relationships—first with Jesus and then with those in His body. Jesus needs to be our primary focus—pleasing Him must be our highest calling and communicating with Him the heartbeat of our existence. Above all else, if we are in love with Jesus, not only individually but corporately, then our expressions of church are likely to be healthy and vibrant.

In Ephesians 4:14-15, Jesus is described as the head of His church. In Matthew 16:18, Jesus says, "I will build my church." Too often, Jesus is head of His church in name only. We call Him, "Lord! Lord!" but actually don't give Him real power to impact what happens in His body (see Matthew 7:21). We don't consult Him on decisions, even though they are made in His name.

A. W. Tozer writes, "The God of the modern evangelical rarely astonishes anybody. He manages to stay pretty much within the constitution. Never breaks our bylaws. He's a very well-behaved God and very denominational and very much one of us, and we ask Him to help us when we're in trouble and look to Him to watch over us when we're asleep. The God of the modern evangelical isn't a God I could have much respect for. But when the Holy Ghost shows us God as He is, we admire Him to the point of wonder and delight."[2]

We have made Jesus impotent as we create our own blueprint for what we want Him to do. But the truth is that Jesus has a master design. If we as individuals and as churches follow His plan for our situation, the Holy Spirit will orchestrate something beyond anything we could ask or imagine. Let's give God His church back! Enough of our programs and plans. It's all about Jesus.

Enough of our programs and plans. It's all about Jesus.

As David has been experiencing firsthand, there is an increase of regional networks springing up spontaneously around the country. Women as well as men are envisioning and equipping people on this journey. These regional expressions may be conferences, Web sites, or gatherings of leaders. They not only serve to train and equip others, but they also give a sense of the bigger picture of what God is strategically doing in an area. The different groups sometimes unite for a social project.

For example, in the Dallas/Fort Worth area, the networks of simple churches are working together to impact a community with one of the highest rates of poverty and single-parent families in the metroplex. They have volunteered to do yard work for the elderly and disabled. They are distributing food, clothing, and toys to needy families. Their efforts are not only helping an impoverished community, but they are also forming meaningful connections among fellow believers from all over the area.[3]

Let's fall in love with Jesus all over again, seeking God's will for us as individuals and corporately for our churches.

10

CHURCH IS BUILT ON RELATIONSHIPS

The Woman Who Was Looking for Intimacy

Just as our bodies have many parts and each part has a special function, so it is with Christ's body. We are many parts of one body, and we all belong to each other. — ROMANS 12:4-5

�֎ In many ways, a house church is like a spiritual extended family; it is relational, spontaneous, and organic. . . . The house church reflects God's qualities and His character. This community lifestyle is molded in the spirit of love, truth, forgiveness, faith, and grace. In house churches, we love each other, forgive each other, mourn with those who mourn, laugh with those who laugh, extend and receive grace, and constantly remain in touch with God's truth and forgiveness. The house church is a place where all masks can be removed, and where we can be open to one another while still loving each other.

— WOLFGANG SIMSON, *The House Church Book*

Please note: Lisa's story is extremely unusual and may challenge your preconceived notions of how God can work. Like the Roman officer Cornelius in Acts 10, Lisa was touched by the Holy Spirit before she had a real relationship with the Lord. And God used a New Age therapist's couch as the place to meet her! God has had His hand on Lisa, moving in unconventional ways to transform her life. God cannot be confined to our theological boxes. As C. S. Lewis says, "Aslan is not a tame lion!"[1]

"HONEY, I MET this guy on the Internet," Lisa told her husband, Kurtis, one day. (For the majority of husbands, this is the last thing they want to hear from their wives!)

"He's talking about intimacy and spirituality in Christian lingo, and the stuff he writes is amazing. I feel like we were put together by God and I'm supposed to be talking with him."

"Well, it's a little weird," Kurtis replied, "and I'm not really sure how I feel about it. But it's okay with me if you want to correspond with him."

But let's back up to the beginning of Lisa's story . . .

For as long as she could remember, Lisa had been searching for something more in her life. She tried to find fulfillment through deeper relationships with her family members, but they did not reciprocate. Lisa thought drugs, alcohol, and sex would fill the void inside her, but none of them made the emptiness go away.

At twenty-one, Lisa became a Christian through a friend's witness. At the time, she was living at home with her mother, after Lisa's father had left the family. Most days, Lisa's mother was depressed and wouldn't come out of her bedroom. In addition to working full-time, Lisa was carrying a full class load at school. Lack of sleep coupled with an unstable home situation took an emotional toll on her. Lisa's friends, also young Christians, didn't know how to deal with everything she was going through.

Lisa also felt alienated at the church she was attending. One day she was so distraught with her problems that she sat outside the church crying. When some church leaders walked by without even acknowledging her, that was the end of that church for her.

There was one bright spot in Lisa's life. She was dating a wonderful man named Kurtis, who was tall and good-looking, and wanted to marry her. He loved everything about Lisa but he didn't want her to push Christianity on him. Lisa loved Kurtis, too, desperately wanting the stability that he could give her. She put her faith on the back burner.

The two married but went through years of counseling; for a while, Lisa was on antidepressants. Lisa was thankful for a good marriage, but she still didn't have the intimacy she longed for. *I guess this is the way my life is going to be,* she thought.

> Lisa decided to see a therapist who specialized in spiritual energy and auras.

Finally, Lisa woke up to the fact that it was time to heal. After trying many conventional methods, Lisa decided to see a therapist named Dave who specialized in spiritual energy and auras. It seemed strange but Lisa was open to anything.

Just before her third session, Lisa sensed something significant was about to happen. She prayed before she went in. "Jesus, will You and God and the angels be there with me? May I know Your love. And please will You heal me?"

This time Dave did something he had never done before. As Lisa was lying on the table, Dave shook rattles over her and told her to let go and fall. Lisa felt as though she was falling through the table, accompanied by high-frequency vibrations.

When Lisa got off the table, the physical sensations she felt were so intense she wasn't sure if she could drive home. The tingling lasted for three days, but the feelings of peace, joy, aliveness, and love were permanent. At first, she didn't know what had happened. But then she remembered her prayer for healing. *It was God.*

Something else Dave had said during the session came back to her. "I have the impression that you are going to meet a man in the future who will change your life. You will be so changed that you will have no words for it—the words won't even be in your vocabulary. And it's going to be soon!"

A Mysterious Connection

Lisa had been reading some books on spirituality and sexuality recommended by a friend. The author did not specifically advocate any particular religion, but the content definitely had an Eastern-religion tone. Impressed with the books, Lisa visited the author's Web site and discovered a bulletin board. Lisa was compelled to post something on the board.

After her second post, Lisa received a personal e-mail from a man named Jay.

"Our greatest desire is for intimacy and our greatest fear is of rejection," Jay wrote. "We have to have other people in order to share love. We cannot do it on our own—there has to be someone else to experience it with."

This was music to Lisa's ears.

Jay mentioned the four different kinds of love—affection, friendship, eros, and charity—that C. S. Lewis explains in his book *The Four Loves*. Jay said that Jesus was a garbage man who could deal with the garbage in our lives.

It had been a long time since Lisa had thought about Jesus or Christianity. Jay's e-mail brought back her negative experiences with

> **Kurtis believed Christianity was too restrictive, with too many rules.**

church; she also knew how Kurtis reacted anytime the subject of Christianity came up. Kurtis believed Christianity was too restrictive, with too many rules. It didn't feel alive to him. Lisa wanted to improve her relationship with Kurtis, not do anything that would distance him from her.

But then she recalled Dave's word to her about meeting a man who would change her life. That's when Lisa asked Kurtis if he would mind her corresponding with Jay.

Lisa and Jay started an e-mail conversation. She learned that Jay was a committed Christian who was concerned for a friend enamored by the spiritual intimacy CDs by the author Lisa liked. Jay found the Web site, and subsequently found Lisa. Two months later, the New Age bulletin board was gone!

One of the first things Jay did was to apologize to Lisa for the church's inability to help her. "I cannot proceed further without asking your forgiveness for what may have been represented to you as 'church.'" He explained that he attended church in a home. "In the New Testament, that was the way church used to be. It's a pattern for us today."

Week after week, in his e-mails Jay would insert Scripture verses that Lisa would look up later to read in context. Then she would e-mail him back with her questions.

The spiritual bond between Jay and Lisa grew. It was very apparent that the Lord had put Lisa in touch with Jay, a Christian for more than thirty years. He never dismissed her experiences as weird or made her feel different or "bad." As the months went by, Lisa began to regard Jay as a "spiritual father." She also began to learn a new vocabulary, just as Dave had predicted. When Jay talked about the Holy Spirit, Lisa remembered the unforgettable physical sensations she had experienced during the last therapy session with Dave.

> Jay apologized to Lisa for the church's inability to help her.

"Whoa, do you think that could have been the Holy Spirit?" she asked Jay in an e-mail.

He wrote back, explaining the concept of *prevenience*— God working in our lives even before we really know Him. "Judging by the fruit in your life, I believe this could have been the Holy Spirit!"

Lisa knew about being "born again" from her first introduction to Christianity and was concerned that her experience was so radically different. She prayed, "God, if that experience on Dave's table was not from You, would You please take it away?"

On January 7, Jay asked her the critical question. "Do you know that you belong to Jesus?"

"I would have to go with my heart and say yes! I'm just sitting here now, feeling a celebration taking place inside me. It's amazing!" she replied.

Lisa wanted to meet other Christians in her city and find a new church home as soon as possible. The first church she thought of was the Church of Faith and Serenity, a New Age church that some close friends attended. She let Jay know her intentions.

Because he knew how important a sound fellowship would be to Lisa's faith journey, Jay scrambled to find an individual or locate a group near Lisa. Jay recalled an Internet simple church database, skimmed it, and came across a telephone number in Lisa's city. When he called the number, he found himself talking with Randy, the leader of a network of home churches in that city! Jay and his wife, Carleen, had met Randy two years before at a conference.

"I think you will find that Randy and his wife will be lifesavers for you," Jay told Lisa.

A few days later Lisa and Kurtis were sitting down at a Starbucks with Randy and his wife, a couple in their early fifties.

The Beginning of Their Spiritual Journeys

As Lisa and Kurtis told their stories to the couple, Lisa described how she and her husband had met weekly for ten years with a group of friends to share about spirituality and how to strengthen their marriages. Randy made a suggestion. "If you get some of your friends together, we could come to your house and meet with you all to discuss spirituality."

That would be wonderful, Lisa thought. In the past, when a group of Lisa and Kurtis's friends got together, the girls would talk about spiritual things while the guys talked cars or sports. Now the only thing she wanted to talk about was Jesus. The idea of a group of people regularly discussing things of the Spirit and building each other up in love seemed incredible to her.

Within a few days, Randy received Lisa's reply. "I would like to have church at my house."

Kurtis wasn't keen on the idea, but he still wanted to be supportive to Lisa. "I'll be there for you, but don't have any expectations for me. I'll just be there."

Over the next few days when Lisa would meet someone, she'd ask the Lord, "Is this someone I should ask to come?" If she heard yes, she invited the person to her home. Actually, she invited just about everyone she met. In the past, Lisa had never felt she had anything in her life worth sharing. But now she couldn't stop talking about what God was doing in her life. Many people who had known Lisa for years could see she was different and were curious about the changes in her life; others were put off by the fact that it was because she was a Christian.

That week about a dozen people, most of them former-Christians-turned-New-Agers, gathered in Lisa's living room. After a potluck meal, Randy began: "Tell us the story of where you are on your spiritual journey."

Each person talked for several minutes about where their lives were spiritually, and about the journey that had led them there. Before

> Many people who had known Lisa could see she was different and were curious about the changes in her life.

the evening ended, they broke into pairs and prayed aloud for each other. It was a deep and meaningful time, and several said they would be back the following week. Randy promised them he would have a spiritual book they could look at together and use as the basis of their discussions.

The next week they again began with a meal together. "What God events happened in anyone's life this week?" asked Randy, starting the discussion. Everyone seemed to have something they could attribute to God and eagerly shared it.

"The book that I want us to look at together is the Gospel of John," Randy explained. "It comes from the Bible, the number one book of all time on spirituality. We will use three symbols to help us in our discussion as we read: a question mark if there is something you do not understand, a lightbulb if the verse sheds light on something going on in your life or you get a fresh insight as to what God is saying in the verse, and an arrow if you sense God piercing your heart with something He wants to say to you. Our discussion will spring from that."

They started their studies in the Gospel of John, taking it a verse or thought at a time. John chapter 1 was a wonderful introduction to Christianity for the group; talking about light and life and other concepts came naturally for them. Randy did not explain the passage to them, but let them explore it together. For example, someone might say, "I have a lightbulb on this verse. Last week at work God showed me how I needed to put this Scripture into action." Each week they spent about forty-five minutes studying a verse or Scripture passage. There were no right or wrong answers, and everyone's opinion mattered. But Randy continually pointed to Scripture as their authority.

> **Answers to prayer frequently became the basis of the "God events" discussion the following week.**

Following the discussion, they prayed for each other. At this stage, Randy was not sure whom these people were praying to, but God delighted to answer their prayers. The answered prayer frequently became the basis of the "God events" discussion the following week.

It took about four weeks for the group to accept the Bible as their authority. By week six, the group had reached a crucial verse: "But as many as received Him, to them He gave the right to become children of God" (John 1:12, NKJV).

"What does it mean to receive Him?" asked Sandy, a

massage client of Lisa's who, with her boyfriend, had been involved in the group almost from the start. Several people contributed their ideas.

"I think it means a commitment," said Traci, a single mom.

After some general discussion, everyone concluded that this was indeed a good definition.

Pat, a friend whom Lisa knew from their involvement together in a community choir, commented, "Commitment is a serious matter. It's like marriage."

"Why don't we each go to a different part of the house on our own and commit our lives to Jesus?" suggested Randy. "Becoming a Christian can be as simple as committing as much as we know of ourselves to as much as we understand of God."

For about twenty minutes, each person spent personal time with God. When they came back, most had obviously had some kind of spiritual experience—there were lots of tears and hugs.

The group has grown much closer over time. Each one of them, including Kurtis, is on the journey of discipleship. Once the group was functioning well after a few months, Randy and his wife stepped aside and encouraged Lisa to lead, under the Holy Spirit's guidance, with another mature Christian couple providing input. Jay also continues to disciple Lisa by e-mail. Nearly five years later, she has grown into a remarkably strong Christian with a deep faith. Through the Lord and those He puts in her life, Lisa has found the love and intimacy she desired for so long.

Church Is Built on Relationships

Almost everyone has a God-given, inbuilt desire for close friendships with people who know them as they really are and who love them anyway. Stories build these kinds of relationships. When we know someone's story, we feel empathy and closeness with him or her.

We have a friend who used to be the pastor of a legacy church in Denver. One afternoon, he sat at a coffee shop with a sign that read, "I'll buy you a cup of coffee if you let me tell you my story about God." Only one person took him up on his offer. The next day he changed his sign to read, "I'll buy you a cup of coffee if you tell me your story about God." This time, people were lining up to spend time with him, many of them ending up in tears. And our friend didn't even have to spend much money on coffee; most people just thanked him profusely for listening to them.

- *Let people tell their stories because stories are powerful.* (Hence the idea of this book!) People love to tell their stories and it often helps you discover what's on their hearts. When we get a group of unbelievers together for the first time, we usually open things up by having each one tell us his or her spiritual story. It gives us a very good idea about that person's spiritual background and beliefs in a nonthreatening way.

When people tell their spiritual stories, you discover what's on their hearts.

- *Tell your own story in a way that doesn't use Christian language, so that it is understandable to the not-yet-believer.* This skill becomes a tool that can be used in multiple situations. It helps build spiritual community and stronger relationships.

- *Share a meal together, share what is going on in your lives, study the Word of God, and pray for one another.* This outline is based on Acts 2:42, where the disciples "devoted themselves to the apostles' teaching and to fellowship, and to sharing in meals . . . and to prayer." It can be used for all your group's times together, whether it is with unbelievers or mature believers. Be sensitive to the Holy Spirit's guidance. For example, one time you may spend the entire time praying for a certain request or situation. But in general, plan on covering each of these areas during the time you are together.

- *Nurture vibrant and loving relationships by caring about each other and sharing your lives together.* In John 13:35, Jesus says, "Your love for one another will prove to the world that you are my disciples." Close and loving relationships are foundational to the DNA of organic, simple churches.

- *Express that love in practical ways.* Church was never meant to be a social club. There are over fifty "one another's" in the New Testament—instructions to love one another (John 13:34; Romans 13:8), serve one another (Galatians 5:13), share each other's burdens (Galatians 6:2), and teach and counsel each other (Colossians 3:16), among others. Obeying these commands is second nature to a small and close-knit community that cultivates a loving atmosphere.

- *Be aware that the resources for the harvest are often in the harvest.* When someone becomes a Christian, it is more effective to help them start something within their circle of relationships rather than invite them to come to your simple church. In Lisa's case, she quickly opened up her sphere of influence for the gospel. With help from more mature Christians, Lisa has been an effective laborer in her harvest field.

11

CHURCH IS FAMILY

The Couple Who Realized That Church Begins at Home

You are citizens along with all of God's holy people. You are members of God's family. — EPHESIANS 2:19

❈ The spiritual DNA of the church will always lead its members toward authentic, viable community. It will always lead Christians to live a shared life through the Holy Spirit that expresses the life and values of Jesus Christ. In other words, it will live as the family of God. In this way, the church becomes the visible image of the triune God. By sharing in the communion of the Father and the Son through the Holy Spirit, the church puts God's love on public display. It becomes His family in the earth in reality.

— FRANK VIOLA, *From Eternity to Here*

THOMAS AND MARIE have a wonderful family. Their two children, Joy and Stephen, love learning about the Lord. But it hasn't always been an easy journey for them.

Thomas and Marie had been attending a megachurch for several years, enjoying the wide variety of good programs offered. Every Sunday, Joy (then age eight) and Stephen (age six) went to their own Sunday school classes while Thomas and Marie stayed in the sanctuary for the sermon.

> "If I hear about Noah and the ark one more time in Sunday school, I'm going to throw up."

One day on the way home from church, Joy made an announcement: "Mom, Dad, if I hear about Noah and the ark one more time in Sunday school, I'm going to throw up."

Marie and Thomas began to pray about finding a new church. Shortly after, the family moved to the country, about forty-five minutes away from the city and their church.

Thomas had worked for a ministry whose goal is to see a church within walking distance of every person worldwide. He was very familiar with the fact that in many other parts of the world the church is exploding with growth because of church-planting movements. (A church-planting movement is a rapid multiplication of churches led by nonprofessional local people within their own culture. This is mainly accomplished through churches that meet in homes.) He had read books by Robert Fitts explaining how simple churches in homes are relevant not only in Eastern cultures, but in Western culture too. As Thomas and Marie discussed and prayed about what to do about church, they concluded that since they were homeschooling their children, a simple, organic church might be best for their family.

Thomas didn't want to do anything without the approval of his pastor. "I really want your blessing," Thomas told him.

The pastor laid his hands on Thomas and prayed, "Lord, I know Thomas, and I trust Thomas. I know that he's Your son and You're calling him to lead a gathering. So I'm going to release him, in Jesus' name, to do this."

Following breakfast on the first Sunday morning in their new home, Thomas sat his kids down on the couch in the living room. He stood in front of them with his Bible held out in his hands, just like a preacher in a megachurch. "Now kids, I want you to turn to 1 Kings, chapter 1." Thomas taught the Scriptures verse by verse, sharing and interacting with his family . . . for four hours! Needless to say, he quickly learned to draw the kids into the discussion.

As the weeks went by, the family covered 1 and 2 Kings and 1 and 2 Samuel. The kids loved the fact that Dad was spending the whole day with them!

That insight made Thomas rethink his understanding of church. It was as valuable for him to listen to his kids as it was to teach them. The kids loved to enter into discussions about the passages Thomas shared, and they memorized lengthy sections of Scripture. They were really excited about church at home.

There was something else the family did that was different. Week by week, they kneeled or sat on the floor, held hands, and asked the Holy Spirit to come and visit them.

Sometimes they would stay there for up to half an hour, waiting for the Spirit to speak. Thomas told the kids, "Anything you hear the Holy Spirit say to you, speak it out loud."

It was as valuable for Thomas to listen to his kids as it was to teach them.

He explained to them that when a person quiets his or her heart before the Lord and asks God to speak, the Holy Spirit will whisper thoughts or bring pictures to mind. The Spirit began to speak to Thomas and Marie through their kids. Sometimes Joy and Stephen saw a picture, or God gave them a Scripture, or they heard a more direct word from God. Then the Lord would give Thomas or Marie a revelation or an understanding of the word from God. Together they learned to allow the Holy Spirit to lead them as a family. The Scriptures began to come alive, not because they were reading them verse by verse, but because God was speaking through them. On occasion, Joy and Stephen even received words of knowledge.[1]

Things continued this way in their little church for a year and a half. Thomas thought that everything was wonderful— and it was. Christ was present in their times together.

One day, Thomas prayed, "Lord, we're really growing as a family now, and I recognize there's more You want me to do. Lord, maybe we need to move on."

God spoke clearly to Thomas's heart and told him he hadn't really learned what it means to live a life in Christ. "You need to listen more to Me and fall more deeply in love with your kids and your wife," God seemed to say.

In retrospect, Thomas sums it up like this: "You can fall so deeply in love with the Father that it flows out of you onto your kids and your wife. Timothy and Titus teach us that the elders of the church have that as the model of their lives. Leadership in the church in North America is based on position, privilege, power, degrees, or going to seminary. The Lord showed me that leadership actually is more like a father giving his life away to his family. As it is in the natural family, so it is in the spiritual family."

Adding to the Family

Three years into this church life, a young couple came into Thomas's office, hurt and brokenhearted. They had just met with the pastor of the megachurch they attended, bringing to his attention some indiscretions in the church. The pastor informed them in no uncertain terms that he didn't appreciate this and asked them to leave the church!

"We are wondering if God wants us to be involved in a home church environment," they told Thomas. The couple, in their early twenties, had only been married for about eighteen months.

Thomas shared with them how his family experienced church. "We would like that. Can we visit you?" the young couple inquired.

"I think you need to go and visit some other folks. We're still pretty new at this. I know of three other groups closer to you who've been established longer," Thomas replied.

Three weeks later the couple was back in Thomas's office. "We still haven't found what you described and we really want it. Can we please come to your house?"

The Lord spoke clearly to Thomas. "Take them home!"

Thomas describes what happened next. "That young couple came and a new ministry began for us. That couple brought another young couple with them, and Marie and I became their spiritual parents. We poured our lives into them and helped them with various issues. They were comfortable in our intimate setting. They referred to our simple church as a safe place—a place where they could open their hearts and not fear that people would gossip about them.

> "Our simple church was a safe place—a place where people could open their hearts without fear of gossip."

We taught them how to bless one another, how to hear God's voice, and how to understand what God is saying.

"For the next three years, I estimate that we had fifty to sixty couples come to our home. Some stayed for a long time; others just visited to observe a simple church in action. Some planted other gatherings in different parts of the country.

"What people find so attractive is the way our family lives. It's painfully difficult to be transparent with family and just as difficult to surrender your life to someone else. But when you do, you see the fruit and it becomes a great joy. As these couples begin to live this way, God attracts other couples to them. The Lord brings those He wants here."

At the Sunday house gatherings, the church members

listen to the Lord and bless each other. Then during the week, Thomas (and sometimes Marie) spends time with people counseling them and doing "life discipleship." The focus is on each person's identity and destiny in Christ, exploring what that means for the person within his or her family, as well as within the context of the community of believers.

Thomas teaches them the principles found in Luke 4:18-19. There Jesus says, "The Spirit of the LORD is upon me, for he has anointed me to bring Good News to the poor. He has sent me to proclaim that captives will be released, that the blind will see, that the oppressed will be set free, and that the time of the LORD's favor has come." Thomas and Marie believe that as these young couples are set free, they will introduce to Jesus others who need to be set free too.

What Spiritual Leadership Looks Like

Thomas has both a pastor's and a father's heart. "For us, the family is the most foundational expression of the church; God wraps around a family other couples who need what they have. It is an expression of John 17:23, where Jesus prays for all His followers, 'May they experience such perfect unity that the world will know that you sent me and that you love them as much as you love me.' When the *oikos* (your sphere of influence) community comes together, this is the primary gathering of church."

Thomas believes that the churches he has helped start will

become more missional, reaching out to the world around them. As this happens, Thomas will hand over the network to the "spiritual fathers" he has trained through life discipleship. He will be a "spiritual grandfather," keeping in touch with those churches and visiting them often, but free to start other networks elsewhere. He is also encouraging the people in his simple church to start their own churches. "It's like kids going off to college," he says. "We're releasing them to start their own spiritual families."

In his experience, Thomas has seen that people who become Christians in a simple church environment usually do so without religious baggage. But there is also a need for house churches that start with people from a Christian background. "We need both kinds of churches," Thomas explains. "There are fifteen to twenty million Christians in this country who have given up on church. If they become healthy, they could lead simple, organic churches, and some of them would lead networks. We need to get them healthy and then release them to bring in as many others as possible!"

Just like Family

In the New Testament, different metaphors are used to describe the church—a body, a temple built of living stones, and most common, a family (Ephesians 2:19). The apostle Paul often refers to himself as a father to the churches he has founded (1 Corinthians 4:15) and to others as his brothers and sisters (Romans 1:13).

Family is not something you go to. Family is something

you are. Getting together doesn't make you a family; it's the relationships that you have with one another.

In a family, life is informal. Can you picture a father talking for an hour at the dinner table without giving his kids time to interrupt? Church is life—family life. And like a family, it is relaxed and casual, adapting to circumstances, allowing conversations to ebb and flow.

> *Family is not something you go to. Family is something you are.*

Like a family, simple churches are constantly developing. In a family, children are born. Older kids get married and move away. Simple church is the same way. Churches come and go, but the relationships remain.[2]

Leadership in the New Testament is clearly described in terms of being a parent rather than being the president of a company. Good parents will do everything they can to help their children grow into maturity. Thomas and Marie are a wonderful example of this kind of parental leadership. They live to serve and encourage others.

In Matthew 20:25, Jesus describes how leadership works in the world. "You know that the rulers in this world lord it over their people, and officials flaunt their authority over those under them." But Jesus continues, "Among you it will be different."

The first-century church had no clergy/laity distinction. Instead there was a genuine priesthood of all believers. There were definitely leaders but their purpose was to equip the people "for the work of ministry" (Ephesians 4:12, NKJV).

Jesus also emphasized that anyone in leadership needs to be the servant of those he leads (Matthew 20:26-27), something Jesus demonstrated when He washed His disciples' feet (John 13:5). In simpler forms of church, leadership is not based on education (except that gained in the school of experience) or on a charismatic personality or on natural ability. Rather, it is based on character issues such as how a person treats his family or whether or not the person is willing to open his or her home (1 Timothy 3:1-13).

I've seen how God is training a new breed of leaders—people who have spent time on the back side of the desert with God, struggling with disappointment and disillusionment. They were unable to hear God or understand what He was doing with them, yet continued to love Him with all their hearts. These are people who have died to themselves and to their own ambitions. They are people God can trust with leadership.[3]

12

THE KINGDOM AT WORK

The Man Who Prayed on the Job

And there were loud voices in heaven, saying, "The kingdoms of this world have become the kingdoms of our Lord and of His Christ, and He shall reign forever and ever!" — REVELATION 11:15, NKJV

☀ For a long time the church has taken care of itself only, but the time has come to take responsibility for every sphere of society, from our circle of friends to our families; from our workplaces to our city councils and schools; from sports and the arts to politics and business. Today the church needs to bring peoples and nations out of the desert, where they have been wandering. The kingdom of God is God's total answer to man's total problem. It is synonymous with God's will and ways. When He says, "Your kingdom come" (Luke 11:2), it means through you and me.

— SUNDAY ADELAJA, *ChurchShift*

"This is not the kind of professional behavior we expect from our employees! I hate to do this, Joe, but I don't have a choice. You are suspended from work pending further investigation."

The day had started normally. Joe worked for a long-distance telephone company as a team supervisor in their customer service department, managing twenty-five people. Just before lunch, Andy, one of his team members, came to him, looking upset.

"Joe, can I see you for a second?"

They stepped out of Joe's cubicle into the busy hallway where Joe could still keep an eye on his team.

"Joe, please pray for me. My uncle, the one who raised me, has had a severe stroke and he's dying. The doctors want to take him off life support. I'm his only living relative so I have to give my permission. I'm on my way to the hospital now. It's all up to me and I just can't bring myself to do it. If I say they can turn off the life support, he will die. What should I do?"

Tears were rolling down Andy's cheeks and his body shook with sobs. As they stood in the hallway, Joe put an arm around Andy's shoulder and prayed for him in a low voice. "Lord, please help Andy know what he should do. Give him the courage to make the right decision." Joe prayed with him quietly for two to three minutes and then Andy left.

Two hours later, following the regular weekly team leaders' meeting, Joe's supervisor approached him. "I heard you were praying on the floor earlier today. Is that true?"

Joe explained what had happened. But before Joe had time to get back to his desk, the boss of the entire center stopped him.

"Joe, we have a real problem here. Someone overheard you praying with Andy and has complained. We cannot allow you to pray with people on the floor."

"Come on. This is ridiculous!" Joe exclaimed. "I was only trying to help one of my team members who was in trouble."

"We need to hold a further investigation into this matter. As of this moment, you are suspended, with pay, until it is complete."

Joe was devastated. *How am I going to explain things to Holly?* His wife had coped with so much already.

Since the time they had first met, Holly knew she wanted to spend her life with Joe. Three years after getting married, when Holly was twenty-five years old, she became a believer through listening to a Christian radio station and then responding to a pastor's invitation at her mother's church. Joe struggled with the dramatic change in Holly: she was so different from the woman he married. But he still loved her.

"Someone overheard you praying and has complained."

By the time their family grew to five children, Joe was managing a video store. One day, just before Christmas, Joe was at work during an ice storm. As he took out the trash, he slipped and fell on the sidewalk, breaking both his ankle and leg. He was released from the hospital on Christmas Day, but was laid up for weeks at home, unable to get around. To make things worse, Joe lost his job at the video store.

Months passed. One Sunday morning in early spring, Holly said to Joe, "The kids and I are going to church. Do you want to come?"

Holly had asked Joe to come to church with her many times, but Joe had always found an excuse not to go. By this time, he was so desperate to get out of the house that he would do anything, even go to church. So he accompanied Holly and the kids to the simple church they had been attending for about five months.

That Sunday morning, the Lord spoke to Joe. Without anyone preaching or praying with him, Joe surrendered his heart to Jesus.

> The change in Joe's life was immediate. He stopped worrying!

The change in Joe's life was immediate. He stopped worrying! In the past, Joe used to stay up at night worrying about everything. It made Holly think twice before telling him about things. For example, if she was having car problems and mentioned it to Joe, she knew he would not be able to sleep until the problem was fixed.

Shortly after Joe became a believer, the position with the long-distance telephone company opened up. Joe progressed quickly up the company ladder to his current supervisory job. From his first day on the job, Joe didn't hide the fact that he was a Christian. He often had his Bible sitting on his desk. It had never been a problem or interfered with his work before. But now it appeared that because of his Christian faith, he would lose his job. Joe had been with the company long enough to know that people were rarely reinstated once they had been suspended. He wasn't looking forward to the financial struggles that lay ahead for him and his family. But the church prayed that God would work a miracle.

Two weeks later, their prayers were answered: Joe was reinstated. The company's higher-ups had reviewed his work for any kind of impropriety but Joe's record was clean. Legally, they could not fire him.

"We can't fire you for praying," his supervisor told him, "but don't let it happen again! If you come across another situation where you need to pray with someone or comfort that person, you must find a private room and close the door."

"Are you saying that it's not a problem if I meet with people in a private room?" asked Joe.

"Yes."

"How can I get a private room?"

"Put your name on the list to reserve a room, and I'll let you know if one becomes available."

Joe didn't waste any time putting his name on the list. But before long he was so focused on his job that he had all but forgotten about it.

God Works Out His Plans

A few months later, Joe's supervisor surprised him with the words, "We have your room for you." The room was reserved in Joe's name for lunchtime every Tuesday. Immediately, Joe let people know that he would be holding a weekly meeting for conversation and fellowship. (He did not use the word *church* to avoid raising any red flags for management.) He wasn't permitted to put up fliers, but Joe didn't need to—the news traveled effectively by word of mouth.

Interestingly enough, the entire management team of the company was studying John Maxwell's book *The 21 Irrefutable Laws of Leadership* as part of their management development, so Joe decided that he would use that book as his basis for the Tuesday discussions. Maxwell's book is based on biblical principles, so Joe felt he wouldn't be out of line referencing the Bible. The company couldn't disapprove of his group studying one of their own recommended books in greater depth.

A small group of people began to get together regularly on Tuesdays. Then a second "church" met on Mondays, Joe's day off. Joe helped them get started. When one member of the church was transferred to another city an hour away, that person started a church in his new call center.

Then came 9/11.

When news of the attack on the World Trade Center spread throughout the company, Joe and his team were meeting before their shift began. A team member suggested that Joe should pray and before he knew it, a bullhorn was thrust into his hand and he ended up leading the employees on the main floor of the office in prayer. Joe prayed aloud on the company's behalf for the victims of the Twin Towers and their families. When Joe later entered the room for the regular Tuesday lunchtime meeting, it was packed with people. Thirty employees jammed the room, all wanting to pray for the nation. Even Joe's boss was there! Several of the people who attended that day became long-term members of the "church at work."

> On September 11, 2001, Joe led all the employees on the main floor of his office in prayer.

A few weeks later, when Joe was driving home from work, traffic came to a standstill. As Joe was sitting in his car listening to a CD, he glanced in his rearview mirror. He saw the man behind him get out of his car and approach another car. The next thing Joe knew, the man was at his window.

"Do you have a cell phone I can borrow?" the stranger asked.

"Sorry," Joe replied. "I don't carry a cell phone."

The man paused for a moment. "Oh, I love that song!" he said. "It's Dennis Jernigan, isn't it? Are you a Christian?"

The two of them began chatting. "Where do you go to church?" the man asked Joe.

"I go to a church that meets in a home," Joe replied, explaining a little about the concept. "But it's not limited just to homes. I also have a small group that I meet with at my office."

"You can do that?" the man asked, surprised. Joe briefly told him the story about how he started a group at work.

"I could do that too!" the man exclaimed. He was a co-owner of a local business. He and Joe exchanged phone numbers.

A few days later, the man called Joe and asked if he would help him start a meeting at his office. For the next few months on his days off, Joe helped this new group get up and running.

Joe's faithfulness resulted in four new churches.

Three months after making the first room available to Joe for meetings, the company took back the room. For several months the group met at picnic tables until a change in the company's work hours put an end to an organized gathering.

The Woman Who Needed Joe's Prayers

Just as Joe's faith was known at work, everyone knew that Karen, one of Joe's team members, was a Wiccan. Most people stayed clear of her, calling her names behind her back. When Karen started to ask Joe questions about Christianity, he seized the opportunity to let her know that God was real and she was not alone.

> **Whenever Joe told Karen that he was praying for her, she would just look at him as if he were weird.**

"How can you believe that without proof?" Karen asked. "How do you know that it's God working in your life?" Joe replied by turning the question around. "How do you know it was the spell you cast that caused something to happen?"

Whenever Joe told Karen that he was praying for her, she would just look at him as if he were weird.

One afternoon, Joe had a strong feeling that he needed to find Karen and talk. He discovered her sobbing at her desk, distraught over problems with her boyfriend. He sat down and chatted with her, staying there until she calmed down.

"I'm still praying for you, you know," Joe told her as he left.

This time, Karen expressed thanks.

After his conversation with Karen, Joe was off for three days. When he returned to work, Karen was gone. Nobody knew where she was. She never showed up for work again.

Several weeks later, Joe was called to the reception area, where a man was waiting to see him.

"I had to stop by and see you," the stranger said. "I'm Karen's father. I want to thank you for giving me my little girl back!" Then he told Joe what had happened over the past several weeks.

Unbeknownst to Joe, Karen had planned to commit suicide after work on the day that she had last talked to him. She was pregnant and at first she considered abortion as a way to take care of things. But her feelings of despair deepened and she decided that her own life wasn't worth living anymore either. By God's grace, when Joe said he was praying for her, Karen had a change of heart. That night she drove across the country to her parents' home—with the suicide note still in her purse. Her parents were Christians, and with their help she rededicated her life to Jesus.

"You didn't just save my daughter's life," Karen's father said, with tears in his eyes, "but also the life of my unborn grandchild. When I learned I was coming to town on business, I just had to stop by and say thank you!"

The Kingdom Is Wherever You Are

In the Lord's Prayer we pray, "Your Kingdom come. Your will be done on earth as it is in heaven." We pray that the Kingdom of God would be worked out here on earth, in every part of our lives. But then we divide our lives into sacred (what happens when we are at church or when we are spending time with the Lord) and secular (what goes on all the rest of the time). For Christians in New Testament times, there was no such separation.

Joe's story illustrates that from God's viewpoint, there is no difference between sacred and secular. God is as interested in what goes on at work (or during our recreational times) as He is in what happens when we meet together. If we will let Him rule every area of our lives, He is able to assert His Kingdom authority everywhere our lives intersect the world.

God is able to assert His Kingdom authority everywhere our lives intersect the world.

My husband, Tony, frequently saw this happen when he was practicing medicine in England. He would often pray with his patients, and many of them—probably literally hundreds over the years—found the Lord in his office. During one six-week period, a patient became a Christian every day the office was open!

At one point, all the family doctors in the country received a letter from the General Medical Council (the

British medical licensing body) stating they were changing the rules concerning patient confidentiality. Up until that time, if a girl who was a minor wanted contraceptives or an abortion, the doctor was obligated to obtain parental consent (just as he would if she needed surgery for an ingrown toenail). But the letter spelled out a change in the rules. A girl's privacy took precedence; parents were not to be informed about such requests without the minor's consent.

Tony called a few other doctors who were in leadership within CiCP, the organization that he ran, and they all agreed this was not acceptable. So Tony wrote a letter to the GMC explaining that he represented about two thousand family physicians, and that they refused to obey this edict. They were willing to have their medical licenses revoked by the GMC rather than be forced to change their practice of informed parental consent.

A few weeks later, Tony received a conciliatory letter from the GMC saying they had no idea that some physicians felt so strongly about these issues and that they were free to follow their consciences without fear of reprisal. The kingdom of medicine was being brought under the authority of the Kingdom of God!

This holistic approach can be even more far-reaching. God is interested in the redemption of creation (Romans 8:19-21). Our friends in India no longer count conversions or baptisms as their measure of "success." They are more interested in the impact their faithfulness to God has on society. Do the villages where there are believers now have clean water and electricity? Have roads been brought in? Are the people well nourished?

We can have an effect for the Kingdom in whatever sphere we touch and influence—business, medicine, education, media, and so on. Are businesses run by believers known for their ethical practices and social concern? Are Christians in media and the arts representing the King in what they create? Are we involved in areas of social justice—feeding the hungry, housing the homeless, helping the needy?

God wants "the kingdoms of this world [to] become the kingdoms of our Lord and of His Christ" (Revelation 11:15, NKJV). If we are willing to live for the Lord in every sphere of life, we will be amazed at what He does.

13

SERVICE AND STRATEGY

Students Who Brought God's Kingdom to Their Campuses

The Lord now chose seventy-two other disciples and sent them ahead in pairs to all the towns and places he planned to visit. — LUKE 10:1

If you want to see churches planted, then you must set out to plant churches. The same axiom can be taken a step further to say, "If you want to see *reproducing* churches planted, then you must set out to plant *reproducing* churches."

— DAVID GARRISON, *Church Planting Movements*

JORDAN TOOK A deep breath as he knocked on the door of a fellow student's dorm room. He and a few friends were trying an experiment in their residence hall at the University of Texas. As the door opened, a blast of music hit Jordan and a disheveled youth wearing jeans and a T-shirt peered out.

"Hey, my name is Jordan and I live down the hall. Can I take out your trash?"

No answer. Then, "Why are you doing this?"

"We're a group of Christians living down the hall. We follow Jesus, and we think He would probably take out people's trash. We want to serve the people on our hall and get to know them."

"Well, I guess so. I hate taking out my trash. Cool!"

> **"We follow Jesus, and we think He would probably take out people's trash."**

The previous semester, Jordan and another friend who was also a sophomore had decided to get serious about ministering to the people around them. When they heard about a Christian at another university picking up other people's trash to initiate relationships with them, Jordan decided to duplicate the strategy.

About a hundred people lived on their floor in the dorm. The two split up on a Thursday night and went door to door collecting trash, inviting their dorm mates to go bowling later that evening. Fifteen people who handed Jordan and his friend trash bags joined them for a night of tenpins. It was the beginning of a missional community.

Each week, the Christians collected people's trash in the

dorm and looked for others to hang out with. Each week they invited people to play board games, eat together, or get involved with other activities when they finished collecting trash. Several people who didn't know Jesus also collected trash with them, and fifteen or so students hung out with them regularly.

Halfway through the semester, Jordan put up a poster on his door inviting people to a Bible study on the parables and teachings of Jesus. Seven or eight of the people attended. There was no formal teaching; they just read a parable and talked about what it meant and how it could affect their lives. This led to some genuine discussions on the meaning and purpose of life, and several young students were introduced to the Lord.

Campus Strategy

Campus Renewal Ministries (CRM) is a group that works on different campuses around the United States. It is not a campus ministry in itself but works with all the existing campus ministries to help them stay in relationship with one another. CRM promotes 24-hour prayer initiatives and "spark groups," missional communities or simple churches that work to reach out to the different student groups on campus.

At the University of Texas in Austin about forty-five ministries work and seek God together to reach the campus. A building on campus houses the Campus House of Prayer

(CHOP), a 24-hour prayer initiative where students sign up to pray for an hour or more at a time.

Justin, who works full-time with CRM, describes a little of its history at the university.

"In 2000, a group came in to spiritually map the campus, identifying the distinct subcultures on campus. We also surveyed each of the ministries working on campus to see what was happening collectively and which groups the different Christian ministries were reaching.

"The next fall, various campus ministers realized their ministries needed to shift from what we termed a 'come-to' church to more of a 'go-to' church. We started thinking about how that might look and how we could help the different ministries on campus move in that direction. Our vision statement says, 'We want to see a viable Christian community in every college, club, residence, and culture at our university.' That has continued to be the vision statement behind what we do. It hasn't been easy. The first year we did very little, but in the last few years we have made some headway.

"A survey of the campus revealed several hundred different communities on campus. The agency that worked with us on this project came up with eight different cultural profiles of the students—from creatives and gym rats to intellectuals. We find out which colleges within the university tend to have that profile of student, where they live, and where they spend their time.

"Christians live among those groups and hang out with

them, in an attempt to minister to them. The Christian students deliberately go to places where there is no witness yet.

"Most of the Christian students leading the missional communities are committed to different primary churches. But for others the missional community is their church.

> **"The goal is to establish a relevant Christian community for every student to interact with."**

"The end goal for this long-term plan is to have a relevant Christian community for every student to interact with during their four years of college. We now have more than two hundred missional communities (in essence, simple churches) reaching out to the different groups on campus."

Huan

Huan lived in one of the smallest dorms on campus. Three years before, another Christian student who was a resident assistant (RA) in the dorm had invited some of the students to go to church with him. He loved them and spent time with them, and eventually started a small group that came together to study about God.

The following year Huan became an RA, and he took students to this same small group. Since Huan is from mainland China, he worked effectively with other Chinese students. Many of them came to him in despair; the transition to life in the United States was difficult for them. Huan shared with them how hard it had been for him until God transformed his life. He demonstrated his love for these foreign students by sharing his life with them. Every day they ate or worked out together, and on weekends they did different activities together. As Huan shared with them what God was doing in his life, several of the students became Christians.

Huan also befriended a group of Muslim students from Indonesia who, like him, were in the petroleum engineering department. The Muslims were extremely suspicious of Christians but found Huan to be different. Huan loved them and respected them. He knew he couldn't change them, but he faithfully prayed that God would work in their lives, and that they would want to know the God who had made a difference in his life.

> **The Muslims were extremely suspicious of Christians but found Huan to be different.**

A few years ago, another missional community started in one of the university co-ops. The co-ops are run by the students and have no rules; drug use and rampant sexual activity are the norm. As the missional community met and prayed together once a week, they left the door of their room open and people started coming by to hang out. Many unbelievers came to worship, pray, and be prayed for. Again, some students became followers of Jesus.

The Christian group had another radical idea. Knowing that the co-op had a reputation for throwing wild parties—and how they often trashed the premises—the missional community decided to offer their services as greeters, bartenders, and cleanup crew.

That act of selflessness had a profound spiritual impact on members of the co-op. People still talk about it today. And the students in the co-op know the Christians pray on a weekly basis for their neighbors. They know where they can go for prayer or help.

CRM runs an eight-week "spark course" for students planting missional communites. It is obedience based[1] and teaches one key action and paradigm each week. The training is designed to help people live more intentionally and missionally within the group they want to reach. Not all of the groups are full-fledged missional communities yet. Some are comprised of one or two students trying to build relationships, with hopes of generating enough spiritual interest to start a seeker group. But many are catching the vision, and the missional communities are continuing to expand.

Jaeson

Other student groups around the country are seeing God work in similar ways.

Jaeson, a freshman and a new Christian, was sitting in his Philosophy 101 class of several hundred students. "Who here believes that Jesus Christ is the Son of God?" the professor asked.

Jaeson immediately raised his hand. Looking around the room, he was shocked to see only one other person with his hand raised. Jaeson began to pray for hours every day, prayer walking the campus and crying out to God for the more than 28,000 students there.

God soon began to open doors for him—the student government actually sponsored him to hold evangelistic events on campus. Hundreds of students gave their lives to Christ. But afterward few of them became part of a local church. Jaeson began surveying students across different campuses to find out why.

What he discovered was that even though many students were looking for deeper meaning in their lives, most of them thought church was "boring, irrelevant, and hypocritical." Yet at the same time, many of them were hurting and broken, turning to partying, drugs, or sex in an attempt to fill the void in their lives.

When Jaeson graduated, he got a tech job but eventually left to focus on mission work. Studying a variety of church models, Jaeson realized that the simple, relationship-based churches he saw in countries such as China or India where people shared their lives together on a daily basis made perfect sense within a student context.

If an eighteen-year-old, uneducated Chinese girl can plant a hundred churches a year, why can't a college freshman plant a few churches on his campus? he thought.

Jaeson started Campus Church Networks (CCN), a ministry that trains Christian students to start campus churches. If a student can win his network of friends to Christ and start a small church, and that new believer trains others to do the same, it could transform colleges and universities. It also could help with the post-college church dropout problem that often occurs when Christian students graduate—many of them find it difficult to transfer from the vibrancy of a small group of Christian students involved in college ministry to the more staid atmosphere of many legacy churches. With training, students would be ready to start simple churches wherever their new jobs took them.

The students of today are the leaders of tomorrow. If we can reach them while they are in college, they are the ones who will change their communities, cities, and eventually their nations. Many movements of God have started with students. Could He be doing the same thing again?

Service Never Gets Old

The stories of Jordan, Huan, Jaeson, and other students like them demonstrate how selfless service can expand God's Kingdom. Many simple churches start when people find unique ways to serve their communities. Mission Arlington, near Dallas, Texas, is a network of more than two hundred and fifty churches, mostly meeting in apartments, mobile homes, and neighborhoods. Those churches exist because twenty-three years ago a woman, Tillie Burgin, decided to serve the poor in her community and provide for them in practical ways. Tillie helped a woman with her utility bill and met some other practical needs, and the woman invited Tillie to teach John 3:16 to her and sixteen of her friends.[2]

Another growing segment of society that several simple churches around the nation are serving is the refugee population. Most significantly, the church members help the refugees—many from less developed nations—acclimate to life in this country. Practical things we take for granted are often complicated for someone who has never seen it before. For example, a refugee needs to know that a dishwasher is used for washing dishes, not for cooking rice. People who know little or no English often need help with all the paperwork involved in immigration. These tasks can be costly in terms of time and convenience for church members, but extremely effective in spreading the Kingdom. Other simple churches serve the homeless or others who are marginalized from society.

The students' stories also illustrate the importance of working with God's strategy. As CRM expands its ministry to different universities across the nation, they will know when they have accomplished their objectives when each of the groups on the campus they are trying to touch is reached for Christ.

A refugee needs to know that a dishwasher is used for washing dishes, not for cooking rice.

Simple churches are sometimes afraid of strategy because the members confuse it with programs or denominationalism. Yet when Jesus sent seventy-two disciples ahead to all the different places He was going to visit (Luke 10:1), do you think He had a plan? Does He have a plan for the place where you live or work? Is there a specific group He wants you to serve? As we seek the Lord and listen to Him, He gives us His vision and strategy.

Much of the success of church planting movements

around the world comes because the leaders are willing to implement the strategy God gives them. In India, simple church leaders deliberately target unreached villages and unreached people groups to both pray for and work among them. The International Mission Board of the Southern Baptist Convention is seeing multiple church-planting movements emerge in many different nations, in part because they are willing to strategize under God for those nations. We can learn from them.[3]

You can find more information on Campus Renewal Ministries and Campus Church Networks at http://www.campusrenewal.org and http://campuschurch.net.

14

STONE SOUP CHURCH
The Woman Who Contributed Her Unique Gifts

Well, my brothers and sisters, let's summarize. When you meet together, one will sing, another will teach, another will tell some special revelation God has given, one will speak in tongues, and another will interpret what is said. But everything that is done must strengthen all of you. — 1 CORINTHIANS 14:26

✸ The New Testament church meeting depended entirely upon the headship of Jesus Christ. Christ was fully preeminent. He was its center and its circumference. He set the agenda and directed what took place. Although His leading was invisible to the naked eye, He was clearly the guiding agent. In this gathering, the Lord Jesus was free to speak through whomever He chose and in whatever capacity He saw fit. There was no fixed liturgy to tie His hands or box Him in.

— FRANK VIOLA, *Reimagining Church*

KRISTIN WAS SITTING at her computer, going through her e-mails.

"Hey dear, listen to this!" she called out to her husband, Phil, who was fixing dinner in the kitchen. "It's from that home church mailing list I belong to. They're going to start a house church over here on the west side."

Phil walked into the room and looked over Kristin's shoulder as she read the e-mail aloud.

> Greetings,
> We are inviting all those who would like to meet with other people who are interested in forming an expression of God's church on the west side of the river. Some of you may have visited or attended meetings, but have had to travel east to do so. Some of you are curious and have not visited a house church before. This is for everyone. We are not experts, by any means. Just laypeople following a direction we believe God has been calling us to.
>
> We ask that each one come with his or her thoughts, impressions, songs, gifting . . . and we will see what God has to say to us. We are all members, each with a part. Staying with this theme, my husband and I thought we would have a "stone soup" meal. For those of you who have never participated in this type of meal, you're in for a treat.
>
> Here's how it works. We begin with a pot of water and a large (clean) stone. Each person brings his or her favorite vegetable, spice, etc., to add to the soup. The finished product is a unique combination of "favorites." Note: no backyard mushrooms or surprise veggies that may

or may not be edible! Tea and coffee will be provided.
Perhaps someone could bring some French bread.
    Andrew and Allison

"I've wanted to do something like this for a long time. Since we're between churches, it might be worth a try," suggested Kristin.

Kristin had been a churchgoer for many years. But church had become empty and nonrelational for her. Most times she went because she felt she had to. A couple of times she and Phil had dragged their feet so long on a Sunday morning that they arrived at church just in time for the closing prayer!

A few years before, Kristin had read James Rutz's book *The Open Church*. Rutz's idea that a group of friends meeting together over a meal and talking about Jesus is what the New Testament describes when it uses words such as *ekklesia,* or church, made sense to her. What Kristen longed for more than anything was to actually say something, to be empowered to contribute, to discuss the Bible and its challenges. She wanted to be real about her own life and her neighbors' lives, rather than just discuss the Sunday sermon.

> **Most times Kristin went to church because she felt she had to.**

A Pot of Soup and Much More

The following Sunday afternoon, Kristin and Phil arrived at an attractive home a few minutes away from their house.

Andrew and Allison welcomed them warmly and the couple immediately felt right at home. Seven of them gathered together, all total strangers brought together by e-mail. As they each added ingredients to the stone soup, they began to relax with each other, talking and laughing.

A half hour later, sitting around the big dining-room table, everyone enjoyed the steaming bowls of soup and crusty bread, and learned a little about each other's lives. All of them had been Christians for some time, but for various reasons each person had either given up on traditional church or was between churches.

That first afternoon, the conversation naturally gravitated to the question, what does it really mean to be a church?

"Church is different from a Bible study," commented one person.

"We should do more than just look at the Bible. It includes prayer and fellowship too. And we need to be free to share any problems we might have, so others can pray for us."

"Church is not some kind of group therapy session."

"It's not some kind of group therapy session though," said another. "And I think everyone should be able to contribute."

"Yes, everyone was important in the New Testament church," someone else added. "It says that everybody has a part to play and that we all have something different to bring."

"It's kind of like the soup we made tonight, isn't it?" said

Andrew. "With the soup, we started from scratch. Tonight God has brought a group of people together and He can make us into a caring community. Not only that, but whenever we get together, everyone brings a contribution, and the Holy Spirit takes what each person supplies and makes it into a meal to nourish us spiritually."

Thus began the "stone soup" church. The members did not stay strangers for long; the Holy Spirit developed them into a community that loved and cared for each other. Every week, each person brought something for the meal in addition to spiritual contributions; the Holy Spirit spoke through one person and then another. Each person learned to recognize God's whisper in his or her heart. When the Spirit spoke, the person was responsible to share with the group what He was showing them. Sometimes it could be a verse from the Bible or words from a song; it could be a picture (a visual representation of a concept the Lord was trying to communicate) or a prayer request. As they continued meeting, the group learned to overcome their inhibitions and experienced the Holy Spirit orchestrating their times together.

> The group learned to overcome their inhibitions and experienced the Holy Spirit orchestrating their times together.

Not every meeting was exuberant. Sometimes people would crawl in from a long week and expect God to show up. There were even occasions when a person was so tired that he or she would actually fall asleep!

Yet God was present and immediately made the group's

time together meaningful and valuable. The truth is that any other style of meeting would not have been as exciting.

Kristin admits that for the first time in her life she could truthfully say, "I was glad when they said to me, 'Let us go to the house of the Lord.'"

A year and a half later, Andrew and Allison prepared to go to the mission field with the stone soup church's blessing. Not long after, the remaining members of the group decided to disband, each going where the Lord led them.

Each Contribution Is Welcomed

A vital concept of the Kingdom is the priesthood of all believers (Revelation 1:6). In many denominations, this idea is given lip service but is rarely practiced. But God's Word says that all of us are priests, that all of us can minister to the Lord and to each other (e.g., Colossians 3:16; 1 Peter 2:9).

In simple churches, we use Acts 2:42 as our model. The disciples "devoted themselves to the apostles' teaching, and to fellowship, and to sharing in meals (including the Lord's Supper), and to prayer." A "typical" gathering might include a meal, fellowship, time around the Word of God, and prayer.

In 1 Corinthians 12, the apostle Paul uses the metaphor of a body to describe the church (vv. 12-27). Just as a body has many members and each one is significant, so it is with the body of Christ, the church. Each person in the group is important and each person has a different contribution to make. We are not looking for conformity, but rather, a synergistic diversity.

This body of Christ functions like an orchestra, with the Holy Spirit acting as the conductor. The rich sounds of a symphony occur because all of the different instruments in the orchestra play the part assigned to them. If we all play the melody line in church, we may miss out on the magnificent creativity of the bride of Christ.

We are not looking for conformity, but rather, a synergistic diversity.

But Paul also says that weaker members are necessary to the body of Christ and worthy of greater honor (vv. 22-25). The contributions of those who are shyer or more reticent to speak should be given greater attention.

The ultimate head of this body is Christ, and as each person follows the prompting of the Holy Spirit, the body functions as it should. You see, the Lord wants to be more than "the guest of honor" in our meetings. He actually wants to be in control.

If we are not careful, house or simple church gatherings can run like a traditional church meeting. Our friend John White describes that tendency as, "Honey, I shrunk the church." One person leads the worship, another person teaches; the only thing that is different is that the pews have been replaced by couches. A major dynamic of simple church is that the Lord has a plan for our times together. He knows what is going on in people's lives. If we will let Him, He will touch and change people and the world around us.

This pattern is found in 1 Corinthians 14:26: "When you meet together, one will sing, another will teach, another will tell some special revelation God has given, one will speak in tongues, and another will interpret what is said. But everything that is done must strengthen all of you." That is why keeping the church small is so important. In a larger gathering, it would be impossible for everyone to take part.

But how do we follow the Holy Spirit in a gathering?

Let's say that we are in a meeting and someone has just prayed a powerful prayer of praise to God. What should happen next? How can we know what the Holy Spirit wants? In our experience, the best way is to make that person's prayer our own spontaneous vehicle of praise to God. If a verse of Scripture or a song comes to mind, chances are the Holy Spirit is speaking. In other words, if we fully participate in what is going on, the things that come spontaneously to mind are most likely from the Holy Spirit. Expect a variety of gifts of the Spirit—prayer for each other, insights from the Scriptures, and gifts of the Spirit such as prophecy and visions, just to name a few.

Don't be concerned about making mistakes. People must not be afraid to participate because they haven't gone to seminary or haven't been Christians all their lives. The simpler something is, the easier it is to duplicate; the more complex it is, the more difficult it is to replicate. If Andrew and Allison had served a gourmet meal to Kristin, Phil, and the other guests that first week, it would have sent the message, "If you want to start a church, you have to provide a spectacular meal." Instead, the message was, "Open your home and everyone will bring something."

It applies to other areas too. If you have a skilled guitarist who leads the worship, the implication is that you can only multiply the church if you have a good musician.

If one person does all the teaching, you might think you can only start a daughter church if you have a dynamic teacher.

In simple churches, it's rare to have one person stand up front and teach. Instead, the group interactively studies the Scriptures (for example, using the question mark, lightbulb, and arrow described in Lisa's story in chapter 10). Everyone joins in the discussion. Research shows that people remember only about 20 percent of what they hear, 50 percent of what they see and hear, but 70 percent of what they say themselves.[1] When people share what they see for themselves in the Scriptures, they are learning more effectively than when they passively sit back and listen.

The vital thing is that people learn, and that doesn't necessarily happen in a more traditional setting even with an experienced teacher. Often we have had longtime Christians join us and after a few months say, "I have learned more in the past three months than I learned in three years of sermons!"

In simple churches we are trying to simplify how we "do" church so that more and more people can participate. I love what a Filipino church planter says: "I never do anything in church that a one-week-old Christian would be unable to do!" Think of how that applies to our praying (no more five-minute sermon prayers) or to our sharing what the Lord is doing in our lives (no more Christianese).

> *"I never do anything in church that a one-week-old Christian would be unable to do!"*

Simple is not the same as shallow. Some of my most profound spiritual experiences have come in a simple church context. When the Holy Spirit is free to work as He wills in a gathering of disciples, the effects can be far-reaching. On the other hand, simple can be duplicated. If a few easy-to-follow patterns are established early on, then almost anyone can facilitate a time together.

We multiply what we model. Let's keep things simple and multiply rapidly.

15

DISCIPLESHIP AND TRAINING

The Man Who Started a Discipleship Movement

When you produce much fruit, you are my true disciples. This brings great glory to my Father. — JOHN 15:8

☼ We may see a wide variety of so-called Christians, but the Bible recognizes only one kind—disciples. Disciples are those people whose hearts burn with an unquenchable hunger for God, desiring to know Him better every day. They are not perfect, but they love Him and continue to draw near Him to learn how to trust Him more and be changed into His likeness.

— WAYNE JACOBSEN, *The Naked Church*

"YOU'LL COME BACK here!"

Neil was sitting in a meeting in Long Beach, California, when the Lord clearly spoke these words into his heart. Not only did the Lord speak plainly, but He gave Neil an impression of the house he and his family would be living in; Neil knew the exact residence because he had lived in Long Beach for ten years earlier in his life.

Neil grew up on the beach and loved the ocean. He had been a lifeguard for several years in Long Beach but he had moved away and become a pastor in a traditional church.

Over time, Neil's passion for discipleship, church planting, and mission made him rethink his calling to a traditional church. He began training someone with more of a pastoral heart to take over his position as pastor of the church so he would be free to plant churches. He had a vision to multiply small groups in an organic fashion—organic churches. He wanted to work in an urban area with a large university population—a city with a beach for baptisms, of course! Long Beach fit the description perfectly.

Neil had a team of a dozen people and a set of well-laid plans. They picked a location for a coffeehouse that they would use for evangelistic outreach.

The house Neil sensed God had chosen for him and his family became available. He and his wife, Dana, packed up their house and set out with their three kids, Lacey the dog, a cat, a bird, and all their possessions. They were ready to go into the coffeehouse business.

But when they went to pick up the key to their new

house, the owner broke the bad news: "The current tenant has decided not to move."

Neil and his family stored all their possessions in the coffeehouse, then began a series of moves. The family slept on friends' borrowed couches when they could; they stayed at a friend's cabin in the mountains for a couple of days; for two weeks they stayed in a motel room.

One evening while they were still living in the motel, Neil was walking Lacey to their usual spot on top of a hill in the middle of Long Beach. There, surrounded by the sounds of the city—gunshots, cars screeching, people yelling at each other, dogs barking, sirens—he began weeping for the city and the darkness present there.

"Lord of the harvest, send workers to this city and change this place. Carve a church out of the darkness," Neil begged God.

"I did not send you here to start coffeehouses; I sent you to start churches. Find an existing coffeehouse and pray a church into being there," the Lord told him. So much for his team's business plans!

> "I did not send you here to start coffeehouses; I sent you to start churches."

Seven weeks later, the tenant vacated the house. When Neil's family was finally able to move in, someone even paid their motel bill. "It was God's way of teaching us that we had to follow His way rather than pursuing our own plans," Neil says.

One day when Neil and Lacey were exploring their new

neighborhood, Neil saw a coffeehouse four blocks away. He and the other team members started hanging out daily at the coffeehouse—drinking coffee, playing games, listening to people's stories, and praying.

The team members met for church in Neil's home. With a dozen adults, it was already a large group, but without a single new believer. Their mission to the city was clear. Every day, team members spent time at the coffeehouse getting to know the clientele.

The first night that someone from the coffeehouse came to the church, she said, "I go to a large church all the time, but God is here in this place!" The next week the woman brought her best friend, who then brought her best friend, who brought her best friend! One by one people began to come to Christ.

Multiplying God's Way

In just a short time, Neil's living room was filled with both new and older Christians. It was time to find a second coffeehouse.

The new coffeehouse turned out to be the hangout of a witches' coven and various satanic groups, including some who believed they were vampires (some of them drank blood, filed their teeth down, or slept in coffins!). Two churches started from this new place, the second of these in the home of a believer named Michael.

As a younger man, Michael had prayed a "prayer of salvation," but he had never really committed everything in his life to Jesus. Michael had a painting business, but he also had a drug habit that eventually caused him to lose everything. His truck was repossessed, his house was foreclosed, his business went into bankruptcy, and all his employees left. His wife was fed up with Michael and his friends who were doing drugs, dealing drugs at their house, or stealing from them. When she left her husband, he hit rock bottom.

One day at the coffeehouse, a team member told Michael about Jesus. It was the message Michael wanted to hear; he fell on his knees and gave his life back to Christ. Immediately, he began sharing about Jesus with his friends.

A few weeks later, in the ocean on a frigid December day, Michael baptized four new disciples—people who used to do drugs with him. Neil believes the church was born at this point.

Neil intentionally separated the people meeting at Michael's house from all the other Christians. He wanted it to be a church born out of the harvest of Michael's relation-

> **A person at the coffeehouse told Michael about Jesus. It was the message Michael wanted to hear.**

ships. The church was very evangelistic and grew quickly. It was kind of messy; it had no music and Neil was the only mature Christian involved. Everyone else was either a new believer or still a seeker. He tried encouraging a new Christian to lead the worship, but that person quit. So they started without music and with only the friends Michael had reached.

Another church started out of Michael's house in a

low-income apartment complex, but it only lasted about a year. As people became Christians, they moved out because they didn't want to stay in the ghetto.

But in six years, the church in Michael's home has started around thirty daughter churches, several granddaughter churches, and a few great-granddaughter churches. They have trained missionaries and sent them around the United States and to other countries, such as France, North Africa, Kosovo, Spain, Jordan, and Thailand.

Why are these churches multiplying so rapidly?

"Churches with this kind of reproduction are very harvest-oriented," Neil observes. "They start with nonbelievers, and the people who come to the Lord are trained right from the start to reach out to their circle of influence or *oikos*, the Greek word used in the New Testament that is often translated as 'household.' The other major factor is our use of Life Transformation Groups (LTGs). We find these make a big difference."

Life Transformation Groups

Neil developed LTGs when he was in a legacy church. Knowing that disciple making was the key to church growth, he experimented with different methods of making disciples. He used every curriculum he could find on the subject, but he would get bored after the third or fourth time through it. So he developed his own curriculum—and got bored with that even faster!

Neil brought together a group of people once a week to discuss whatever Christian book was new and interesting. He was soon tired of that too.

"What book could anyone read that would transform their life?" he asked himself one day.

At that moment the light went on. "The Bible!"

At their next meeting, he told the three college students in his group to put their other books away. "I want you to read the entire book of Proverbs before we get together again."

"That much in one week? Don't you know it's thirty-one chapters?"

"Yes, the whole book in one week," Neil insisted.

> "What book could anyone read that would transform their life?"

Neil wanted to begin with the book of Proverbs because one of the young men he was working with was an extremely angry person. None of the other books they had been studying addressed that problem, whereas the book of Proverbs talks a lot about foolishness and anger.

As Neil himself read through Proverbs, he realized how powerful it was to read the entire book in one week. As he read, he designed symbols to identify what the verses were about. For example, if the verse was on money, he put a dollar symbol beside the verse. If it was on communication, he drew a tongue, or if it talked about anger or violence, he drew a pair of angry eyes. The book of Proverbs came alive to him.

When the group got together, the students admitted that they had read only six or seven chapters.

Neil explained how using the symbols had made the difference for him. "You need to try this; it's powerful!" Neil told them. "Let's start again at chapter 1 and read it all the way through this week. Try using these symbols."

> As Neil read, he designed symbols to identify what the verses were about. The book of Proverbs came alive to him.

Neil read the entire book again the next week. He gained even more insights and couldn't wait to share with his students again. This time, no one had read even ten chapters.

"Okay, we're going to keep reading Proverbs until we all finish it in the same week," Neil announced, his frustration evident.

Then it dawned on him: "That's not a bad idea!"

At the end of four weeks, they had all read the entire book of Proverbs in one week. Neil had read it all the way through, four weeks in a row, and it was changing him.

"I found wisdom pouring out of my life in every kind of situation," he says.

But he recognized that the one student still had an anger issue. Neil decided it was time to move on to the book of James, which also addresses anger.

"Let's read James seven times in one week. That's once a day," he instructed the group.

After reading the book of James forty-eight times, the angry student left the group. But there was another student, Kent, who had a drinking problem. At the age of twenty, Kent already had a DUI on his record. He had been involved in an accident and his license had been revoked. His life was circling the drain before he gave his life to Christ. He immediately took to the Word and began to grow. Then came the week they were supposed to read through the book of Romans twice in one week.

"Did you read Romans through twice?" Neil asked Kent at their regular weekly meeting.

"No, I didn't finish it," Kent said. But he had a smile on his face.

"How far did you get?"

"I read it all through once, and the second time through I read fifteen and a half chapters."

"But Kent, why didn't you finish the last chapter? Romans is only sixteen chapters long!"

"Because I want to read it again!"

What a change! This is a young man who spends hours in the Word and he is growing and being transformed.

One day, Neil went alone to the restaurant where the group usually met. He sat down at a table and pulled out his Bible to spend some time with the Lord.

"You should be really proud of Kent. He's doing great with his group," Mary, a waitress, said to him. (She would later become a Christian.)

"Kent has a group?" asked Neil.

"Yes, every Monday morning he meets with a bunch of people here. I remember the 'before' Kent—before you started meeting together; the 'after' Kent is quite a change!"

Neil was astounded. "Kent has a group? Kent has a group!"

Neil called Kent. "What's this I hear about you having a group?"

"I just started doing with some of my other friends what you do with me," he explained.

Kent's group grew into a larger group that broke into several smaller groups. Those groups then continued while Kent started another group in a different place with different people.

> "I remember the 'before' Kent—the 'after' Kent is quite a change!"

Scripture reading, a list of accountability questions that Neil had written, and prayer for nonbelievers form the foundation for the Life Transformation Groups. They have been used throughout the world to make disciples, leaders, leaders of leaders, church planters, missionaries, and pastors. LTGs are one of the main reasons that Michael's church grew so rapidly. From the start, the new Christians were reading large quantities of Scripture (or listening to an audio version, if literacy was a problem), praying for their friends, and confessing their sins to one another.

Mentoring and Training

Neil devotes his life to creatively overseeing the reproduction of healthy disciples, leaders, churches, and movements, so leadership and training are second nature to him. In the traditional church he was part of, he created a leadership development system for training leaders within the context of the local church. But after it was published, the Lord spoke to him.

"I want you to do it again from scratch, but with new converts this time."

When Neil moved to Long Beach, he wasn't interested in starting churches as much as he wanted to create leadership farm systems.

"I wanted to produce leaders that would start organic churches that develop into movements," he explains. "That involves mentoring and coaching church planters out in the field and creating resources to help them while they are on the job. That's how 'Greenhouse' started. My coworker Paul worked with me from the beginning to develop leadership farm systems for those starting organic churches. What has emerged is two weekends of training along with local monthly meetings. We have related everything to the principles used in gardening and farming—hence the name Greenhouse. We even use the term 'organic church' rather than house church, which has too many negative connotations in this country. People tend to associate that term with a small, inward-looking group of disgruntled Christians rather than a vibrant and missional church.

"Mentoring is very important in raising leaders for the harvest. Organic mentoring is dictated by the needs of the person being mentored, rather than a program designed by the mentor. I find that early on, a new Christian is eager to be mentored, but he hasn't done anything yet. I don't spend a lot of time with him at this stage, but I throw out the challenge for him to do something in ministry. I'll spend time with him informally at church; then when he becomes fruitful, I will take more time with him.

"If I find someone very excited about serving the Lord, I'll say to him, 'Go and win someone to Jesus and start an LTG with him.' When they have done it once, I tell them to do it again. They can multiply these groups and start a church. At this point, when they have followers, I will mentor them. The mentoring process at this stage occurs once a week or every other week. As they grow more and more fruitful, they become more time conscious, and they mentor others. Then I shift to mentoring them once a month and coaching them quarterly. Finally I will say to them, 'Just call me if you need something or if a crisis arises.' Or maybe I will bump into them at a conference and spend time with them. It's a layer-upon-layer progression as they begin to invest in others and become less and less needy and dependent on me.

"It's a very organic process based on the needs of the person being mentored. A cookie-cutter approach doesn't work because people are different. But we had no way of knowing that until we got out there and got our hands in the soil.

"Many years ago we tried to start a church using conventional church growth methods. We produced a full-color brochure that went to thousands of homes in a new community. We had a worship band and did everything right. But it failed, and we realized we had not been planting a church, but were trying to buy a church.

"When the LTGs started, we realized we were planting

seed. It was a much more organic approach to raising leaders for the harvest. Mentoring waters that seed so it can bear much fruit.

"Greenhouse teaches that the best soil in which to plant seeds is where people are most needy. 'Bad people make good soil—there's a lot of fertilizer in their lives!' So we need to be out in the fields, where the soil is good, planting seed. The seed of the Kingdom is the Word of God. We are looking for a 'person of peace,' someone who will open up his or her circle of influence to us and who will be the laborer within that people group."

> The best soil in which to plant seeds of faith is where people are most needy.

Greenhouse itself is producing an abundant harvest. Since 2000, Neil estimates that Greenhouse has trained 21,000 people from forty-five states and more than thirty countries in the principles of starting organic churches. Last year they averaged a weekend training every week somewhere in the world with over fifty trainers involved in teaching the principles. At least 20 percent of those trained go on to start a church. Greenhouse estimates that they are seeing more than a church a day as a result of the training. (This does not take into account all the daughter and subsequent generation churches that are starting too. When these are taken into account, that figure rises to more than two churches per day worldwide.)

In 2007, Ed Stetzer conducted a survey of some of the leaders who attended the Church Multiplication Associates (CMA) annual conference. Of the churches surveyed, there was almost a 100 percent rate of reproduction—these churches were producing daughter churches. Around 25 percent of the growth was through new believers.[1]

Discipleship and Training

Nowhere in Scripture does Jesus tell us to plant churches—He tells us to make disciples (Matthew 28:18-20). And when we do, church happens. As Roger Thoman says in his blog,

> When I reach and disciple a viral discipler, that person is going to gather with other viral disciplers for encouragement, and then, as each of them reaches others, still more gatherings will take place. So, along the way, house churches are started. But rather than being the end game, they become a means to support the life that is being reproduced from one disciple to the next. The house church gatherings themselves will shift, change, morph, end, and re-establish themselves in new forms but *the movement of disciples who are reproducing disciples will continue.*[2]

LTGs are a pattern, not a program, of discipleship that produces outstanding results in people's lives. But more than that, anyone can start one! Their genius lies in their simplicity. Research conducted by Kent Smith of Abilene Christian University in 2003 showed that churches, whether legacy or simple, that also encouraged very small groups (two to three people) grew stronger and multiplied more rapidly than those that did not.[3]

Discipleship and training are important. Jesus spent much of His life with only twelve men. He lived with them, ate with them, and shared His heart with them. They saw Him cope with every kind of person and situation. Much of the discipling process consisted in answering their questions. He gave them tasks to do and instructions on how they were to be done and then asked them to report back to Him. He used their experiences for further training (Luke 10:1-23).

New Christians do not need mere head knowledge. They do not need our Christianity 101 courses. They need to become followers of Jesus. John 17:3 says, "And this is the way to have eternal life—to know you, the only true God, and Jesus Christ, the one you sent to earth." As the new believer spends time with us in the presence of the Father, he will learn to know Jesus and how to recognize His voice. As she studies the Word with us, she will catch our hunger and love for the Word. As he watches us pray with others for their needs to be met, he will gain faith to go and do the same. The important thing is that he or she is constantly pointed to Jesus as the model.

New Christians do not need mere head knowledge. They need to become followers of Jesus.

The second part of Luke 11:23 (NKJV) says, "He who does not gather with Me scatters." A friend of ours in India tells of some interesting research. When a major evangelistic crusade comes to an Indian village, hundreds of people may become Christians. However, if you follow up a year later, the churches haven't grown. Instead, the

Indian temples, which may not have had much activity prior to the crusade, have all increased and become livelier. It's as though people have become more spiritual, but because they have not been gathered into communities, the end effect has been to scatter them.

An important part of the follow-up for new believers is that they are gathered into small communities where they can grow. It may be as simple as two or three sharing their lives together in some kind of accountability group where they read (or listen to) Scripture, share their struggles, and pray for their friends. This provides a safe place from which the new believer can be encouraged to reach out to his or her old friends. New wine needs new wineskins.

Visit http://www.cmaresources.org for more information on Life Transformation Groups and Greenhouse training.

16

KINGDOM FINANCES AND KINGDOM KIDS

The Couple Who Believed God Uses Money and Children

You must each decide in your heart how much to give. And don't give reluctantly or in response to pressure. "For God loves a person who gives cheerfully." And God will generously provide all you need. Then you will always have everything you need and plenty left over to share with others. As the Scriptures say, "They share freely and give generously to the poor. Their good deeds will be remembered forever." For God is the one who provides seed for the farmer and then bread to eat. In the same way, he will provide and increase your resources and then produce a great harvest of generosity in you.

— 2 CORINTHIANS 9:7-10

But Jesus said, "Let the children come to me. Don't stop them! For the Kingdom of Heaven belongs to those who are like these children."

— MATTHEW 19:14

✸ The key is in listening to the heart of our Treasurer. Are we in a season of giving or receiving? Chances are we will each experience both seasons moving back and forth from one to another often throughout our lifetime. We need to have "ears to hear" our Treasurer. When it is time to give He will let us know and He will make certain the funds are there to obey His directive. When it is time to receive He will tell us to set aside our pride and accept His grace.

— BILL HOFFMAN, HOUSE2HOUSE WEB SITE

✸ Children are a natural and important part of [the house church] body. . . . Children humble us with their questions, break up our endless "adult" discussions, bring us down to earth from our pious clouds, and act as natural evangelists and bridge-builders. They also help us to prove the fruits of the Spirit—patience, for example— and serve as heaven-sent spies to spot instantly any trace of religious superstition and hypocrisy. Children have a ministry to us adults that is at least as important as our ministry to them.

— WOLFGANG SIMSON, *The House Church Book*

It started with a conversation on a Sunday morning. People were filing out of the beautiful sanctuary of the thousand-member church after the service. Jim, an elder in the church, and his wife, Cathy, were approached by Doug and Ellen, a middle-aged couple and good friends who had also been involved in the church for a number of years.

"Hi, Doug. Hi, Ellen. How are you doing?"

"I was hoping to see you," Doug said. "Do you have a minute?"

"Sure," replied Jim, noticing that they looked a bit anxious. "What's on your mind?"

"Well, it's like this. As you know, I got laid off from work three months ago, and I haven't had a paycheck since September. We've run through all our savings and the credit card is maxed out. And Christmas is coming up! I can't pay the bills, let alone have anything to go toward Christmas. I was wondering if maybe the church could help tide us over. We would only need a few hundred dollars. What do you think?"

"Did you submit the paperwork requesting consideration for benevolence?" asked Jim.

"Yes. I filled it out a couple of weeks ago, but I haven't heard anything yet."

"I'll look into it for you."

Jim knew that Doug and Ellen were not the only ones in financial straits going into the Christmas season. But he was a little skeptical about whether or not the church could help. As part of the church's leadership team, Jim knew a major focus of the church was the management of its money. The leadership meetings were more about raising money than they were about ministry, and all of the money seemed to go to the new building and the full-time staff's salaries.

At the leadership meeting the next evening, Jim brought up Doug and Ellen's situation.

"I'm sorry, Jim, but we just don't have any spare money available to give to this kind of need," the pastor said.

"But our budget is over one million dollars! And these people have been faithful members for many years. I'm certain that they have tithed regularly. Surely there's some cash somewhere for them," Jim protested.

"We do not have any funds to help them," the pastor insisted.

Jim was unsettled when he left the meeting that night. *This can't be right. Isn't the church supposed to be helping its members who are in trouble?* he thought as he drove home. Fortunately, Jim was part of a small group that was able to assist Doug and Ellen.

But the questions kept running through Jim's mind. "What is the church?" he asked the Lord. "I don't want to participate in a church that can't help its members. Please show me what a church is supposed to be."

Jim is a successful businessman, but the economics of his large church didn't make sense to him. So he reread the New Testament, particularly the book of Acts, to see how finances were managed in the New Testament church.

A few evenings later, Jim and Cathy were relaxing over a

cup of coffee. "In the New Testament church, no one had a need,"[1] he told Cathy. "If anyone had anything extra, they brought it to the apostles' feet, and it was distributed to those who had needs."

"So all the money didn't go to buildings and salaries," Cathy commented.

"Take the apostle Paul. In the first letter to the Thessalonians, it records that rather than take offerings from the believers, Paul worked day and night[2] so that he could be an example for them," said Jim. "He wasn't a financial burden to the church at all. Paul was bivocational; he worked as a tentmaker and a missionary. In Asia, he paid not only his own way, but also his team's way."[3]

> "In the New Testament church, no one had a need. If anyone had anything extra, it was distributed to those who had needs."

"There must be some kind of ministry that models what Paul was talking about," Cathy said.

"Yes, I think so. For the first time I'm seeing phrases in the Scriptures like, 'Greet the church in *so-and-so's house.*'"[4]

"So the early church used to meet in people's homes. But there are no churches that meet in homes these days."

"I don't begrudge the time we've had at our church. We've become stronger in the Lord there. But because of their attitude toward finances, I don't see how we can continue going there," said Jim.

"Maybe we could start meeting in our home and see what happens."

Generosity 101

A few weeks later Jim resigned as a church elder. He and Cathy started holding church in their living room with their six kids. Initially, they didn't approach home church as following the New Testament model or even as a better way to minister to people, but strictly as a financial model that made more sense. It did not take long before their kids' friends joined them. At a certain point in time, the group started to collect offerings. When they incorporated as the Association of House Churches, it was with the understanding that anyone joining or leading a house church was committed to being bivocational—working in a secular job as well as serving the church. The only person who was paid a salary from the church was a part-time administrative secretary.

"We came up with a mission statement based on economics," says Jim. "It says 'We will become a thousand-member church meeting in fifty to eighty homes, with 80 percent of our money going to benevolence and missions, both local and foreign.' We are not yet a thousand-member church, but we have honored the financial part.

"Over 80 percent of the money that is given goes to helping people and missions. We support eight local missions in our city and are involved heavily in India. We give to missions in Haiti, and we help some of our people who go on short-term mission trips. And, of course, there is benevolence. We feel we have a church where no one is in need, because if anyone does have a need or an emergency crops up, we have money budgeted and set aside to help them. We're able to help not only people in our own fellowship, but others they may know who have financial needs.

"For example, recently we heard of a single mother who was unable to pay her rent and had fallen behind on her car payments. She was one day away from being evicted, and had gone to a number of churches and different agencies for help. Each one turned her away. We sent a friend of hers over with a pizza and a check to cover her rent. After they visited, the woman disappeared into her bedroom, then emerged with a sheet of paper. It was a suicide note. Our ability to rapidly deploy funds had literally saved a person's life!

"Another family recently immigrated from a Muslim country. When the sponsoring family ran out of money to support them, the foreigners were living in an apartment with no furniture, no money for food or clothes, and no prospects for work. The Muslim groups the family had approached for help had counseled them to return to their home country. The simple church network became aware of this family's situation through a volunteer at a local crisis pregnancy center.

"She contacted a Christian church that worked with similar immigrants in another city and they offered to help this family too. Within a few days, they had a house full of furniture, food, and clothing. Touched by the kindness of the Christians, the Muslim family asked us to pray that the husband would find a job. He is now working. As other needs arise, we pray with them. This Muslim family has acknowledged that it is prayer in Jesus' name that has brought about these wonderful changes in their lives.

"In the beginning, we made financial commitments of a certain dollar amount per month to different ministries. But then we found ourselves in a situation similar to that of many churches. If our giving was down for any reason in one month, we were stretched to meet our commitments. So ten or twelve years ago, we went to a model where we break our giving into percentages. Whatever comes in each month goes out. For example, instead of giving $250 per month to one ministry, we'll give 5 percent of what comes in to that ministry. It has enabled us to increase our giving to different ministries because the percentages have grown as the fellowship has grown. And the ministries pray for us because as the Lord blesses us, we in turn pass it on."

The association has had a positive effect on their city. They are the only churches supporting certain secular ministries that help people in their city. For example, only two groups give on a monthly basis and volunteer at a mission that feeds one hot meal a day to the homeless—one is the Association of Home Churches, and the other is a nightclub, Dan's Biker Bar. Working alongside the staff of Dan's Biker Bar has enabled the home churches to interface with people who never will wind up in legacy-model churches.

> **Over seventeen years, this small network of simple churches has given away more than one million dollars to missions and benevolence.**

"When we first started, no one knew what a house church was," explains Jim. "There was a lot of suspicion, especially among the other churches in our city. Their leaders would ask, 'Who is your ordained pastor and to whom are you accountable?' But our giving has brought us real credibility in the community. We support the crisis pregnancy center, the mission soup kitchen, a homeless center, and a local drug and alcohol rehab center. Some of them are Christian-based and others are secular-based ministries.

"Our support for church planters in India has helped more than four hundred church starts. The ministry we have worked with uses more of a traditional model. But we are now partnering with someone who is establishing a more rapid house church planting model. We often send people to India, but they pay their own way."

Over the past seventeen years, this small network of simple churches has given away more than one million dollars to missions and benevolence.

Empowered Kids

When Jim and Cathy meet people who are new to house churches, they tell them two things: "More people meet in homes than in church buildings worldwide," and "One of the things we value most is the effect of this model on our kids." They have six kids, and all of them except the oldest have been raised in this model of church. All of them either are—or have been—in leadership at one time or another.

"Children are not spectators, but part of the church. They are the church! It's not just our own kids; others growing up in this model recognize they are the church. They don't just come to watch, but are actively involved in every level of ministry.

"During our times together, we purposefully go out of our way to have the kids participate as much as possible. They have the same Holy Spirit, and they are as much a part of the meeting as the adults. If they can read, they'll read some Scriptures, or they may pray with someone or choose a song.

> Kids have the same Holy Spirit, and they are as much a part of the meeting as the adults.

"We may have the younger ones in a separate room with someone older supervising them during the Bible discussion time. But as soon as they are old enough to comprehend, they participate. Once they are old enough to read, they can participate.

"Some visitors came recently, and we all gathered around one individual to pray with him. The visitors were astonished at the mature prayers of the eight-to-twelve-year-old kids. They were praying in the Spirit and interceding dynamically over this individual. We see that kind of maturity at a young age because we purposefully direct our focus to the kids. They know they are as important as the adults. Adults aren't the only ones who hear from God—kids do too!

"A word from God given by a kid has even pushed a meeting in a particular direction. We just ask the kids, 'What do you feel the Lord is saying?' They can talk just like anyone else and whatever they say is valued. Kids are very sensitive to the Holy Spirit. When our youngest daughter was a senior in high school, she had already led a number of people to the Lord.

"We have seen people who haven't stayed with the simple church model because a bigger church has more activities for their kids. They have youth programs and Sunday schools. The family may come for a few meetings and not really participate, and then they go back to the traditional church.

"But the number one benefit for us has been to see what has happened to our kids. As they have grown into their teen years and gone on to college and beyond, they aren't content to be mere spectators. Because our kids have never been shuffled off as unimportant, they have been energized from an early age. And now they are leaders in whatever situation they are in."

Kingdom Finances and Kingdom Kids

Whenever we tell someone we are involved in a network of churches that meet in homes or anywhere people live, it's usually not long before they ask one of three questions.

What happens with finances?
What do you do with the kids?
How do you prevent heresy?

Jim and Cathy's network of churches answers those questions well.

First, because simple churches do not have buildings to maintain or salaries to pay, they do not have to focus on acquiring funds in order to survive financially. Instead, they are able to give the majority of their finances directly into missions or benevolence. That's great news, especially in these difficult economic times.

Simple churches do not have to focus on acquiring funds to survive.

A recent survey of people in simple churches conducted by Steve Lyzenga from House2Harvest showed that more than half of those who responded gave more than 10 percent of their income to charitable purposes. (Compare this to the typical American Christian, who gives about 3 percent to charity.)[5] He also found that 74 percent of simple churches are spending 5 percent or less of their income on internal costs, leaving 95 percent or more of the money they collect to go to benevolence and missions.[6] (The typical institutional church spends 85 percent of all of its funds for the internal operations of the congregation, including staff salaries, building payments, and utility and operating expenses.)[7]

Second, a parent has the primary responsibility to train kids spiritually. It isn't something to be delegated to a Sunday school. Obviously, being part of a community of believers helps tremendously. It's critical to include kids in everything possible. As Jim and Cathy say, "They do not have a junior Holy Spirit; they are the church."

In many simple churches, the kids choose the songs. If the church is going to pray for someone, kids will join in laying hands on that person and praying for him or her. When a child's contribution is valued, he or she will take part in most of what goes on. Simple churches differ as to the logistics of what happens if there needs to be a serious time of adult discussion or study. Some keep the younger kids in the same room—they may color or do some other quiet activity. Others will arrange for the younger ones to participate in more age-appropriate activities with an adult or older teenager in another location. Jesus knows what is best for our kids, and if we ask Him, He will lead us to do what is best for everyone.

Finally, in answer to the third question, "How do you prevent a church from moving into heresy?" we begin with a question of our own—where do most heresies begin?

Most heresies that have gained a grip on a church have occurred when a major charismatic leader starts promoting his ideas. A small group meeting in a home is not likely to create such a scenario. In our experience, if Scripture is emphasized as the authority instead of the person leading the group, heresies are unlikely. The rest of the group makes the necessary corrections.

17

TO TRANSITION OR NOT TO TRANSITION?

The Pastor Who Brought Healing to the Business Community

No one puts new wine into old wineskins. For the new wine would burst the wineskins, spilling the wine and ruining the skins. New wine must be stored in new wineskins. But no one who drinks the old wine seems to want the new wine. "The old is just fine," they say. — LUKE 5:37-39

☼ God is doing all kinds of amazing things with both legacy and simple churches. We are now aware of a number of situations where God has led a legacy church to successfully become a network of house churches. The process has plenty of challenges. Most people who attend a legacy church signed up for a certain form of church, and the changes leave them feeling very insecure. . . . It is best to count the cost before moving ahead (Luke 14:28-32). In other situations, legacy churches are encouraging their members to start simple churches as a means of outreach. . . . God knows your situation! He has a plan that is unique to your circumstances, and He is waiting to reveal His will to you.

— TONY AND FELICITY DALE AND GEORGE BARNA,
   The Rabbit and the Elephant

I LIKE THE way this man thinks. Allen was attending an invest-ment seminar and was particularly impressed by a presenta-tion on how to strategize for tax savings. So he approached the speaker when the seminar was over.

"How can I get you to work for me?" Allen asked.

"I charge $200 per hour, or you can join my business club," he replied.

Allen joined the business club, thinking he would have the opportunity to rub shoulders with other people involved in investing. They met in a nearby city every Monday night for a meal and discussed a topic brought up by one of the mem-bers, before moving to the subject of finances and investing. After a couple of weeks, Allen noticed that the members' input on the general topics often had a New Age emphasis.

What am I doing here? Allen wondered one evening dur-ing the discussion. When he prayed about it later that night, it became clear. "These people are searching for God! Hey, there could be an opportunity here." So Allen began praying that God would open a door for him to share his Christian beliefs at subsequent meetings.

It wasn't long before an opportunity presented itself. At one of the meetings, a lady began talking about the Bud-dhist concept of feng shui, which teaches that how things are placed in an office brings harmony to the room and can bring blessings to a business.

How can I counteract this? Allen thought to himself quickly. The woman remarked how certain buildings feel dark and heavy. At the break, Allen went up to her.

"Your comment about buildings feeling dark and heavy is really interesting. I've also experienced that, but my way of dealing with it is probably a little different," he said.

"What do you do?" she asked.

"I pray over the place in the name of Jesus and command the evil forces to leave," he replied.

The shock registered on the woman's face was obvious; she quickly turned away to talk to someone else. But as she did, a smartly dressed woman in her early fifties stopped Allen.

"I couldn't help overhearing what you were saying," she said. "My name is Linda, and I'm in real estate. I have this house that I just haven't been able to sell. I'm sure there's something dark in it. Would you come and clear it out for me?"

> "Your comment about buildings feeling dark and heavy is really interesting."

"I could do that."

The next day, Allen met Linda at an older house. It was empty except for a table and four chairs in the dining room. He noticed that Linda was carrying a bag of candles.

Oh no, she thinks we're going to have some kind of a ceremony, thought Allen.

"Thanks, Linda, but the candles won't be necessary," he said. "I'm going to pray over every room in the name of Jesus."

Room by room, Allen commanded the darkness to leave and invited the presence of the Lord to come in. As he prayed through the house, Linda was very quiet.

Does she think I'm nuts? Allen finished praying though the main-floor rooms and in the basement. On his way upstairs, he heard the doorbell ring. Linda went to answer the door, while Allen continued praying in the second-floor rooms.

When he came back down, one of Linda's clients was with her. Linda made the introductions, telling the man, "Al is clearing out my house. Doesn't it feel better already?"

> "I'm going to pray over every room in the name of Jesus."

The three chatted for a few minutes and then Allen said, "Linda, can I pray for you too?"

She sat down in a chair and Allen laid his hands gently on her shoulder and started to pray softly. As he did, the Holy Spirit came and Linda started to shake and cry.

Something is happening here. Allen immediately began to pray for the darkness to leave her. When he finished, Linda had quieted down, then said, "I haven't felt so light in years! Can we go for coffee?"

Linda's client had been sitting on a chair in the corner, watching Allen and Linda with a bewildered look on his face. The three of them—Allen, Linda, and her client, a Jewish man—headed for a coffee shop. For two hours, Allen answered their questions about what had taken place at the house. He explained to them about the Kingdom of God, salvation, and forgiveness.

The Holy Spirit Gets Down to Business

The next week at the business club meeting, Linda spotted Allen across the room and ran over with a big smile on her face.

"Al, you have to get on the speaking roster at the club. You have to tell them everything you told me last week."

Allen wasn't sure what to do. But he decided to talk to Susan, one of the organizers of the meetings. Just then a woman walked through the door with a cane.

"What's wrong with Jane? Why is she walking with a cane?" Allen asked Susan.

"She has a problem with her leg that won't heal."

"You need to let me do some teaching on healing."

"We could do that," Susan replied.

The following week, Allen sent Susan an e-mail explaining what he would like to do. "I will share some stories of healings that I have seen, including my wife's back. I'll share how I was introduced to healing and where I'm coming from. Then I'll do a clinic and pray for people."

Allen was surprised when he received a telephone call from Susan later that week. She explained that the speaker scheduled in two weeks had cancelled. "Could you fill that slot?" she asked. He agreed.

When the evening finally came, Allen was terrified. As usual, the group meeting started with a meal, and then one of the organizers introduced Allen.

"As you know, in this club we believe in having an open mind. I don't necessarily agree with religious things, but we have a man of the cloth here with us tonight," said the emcee.

Allen stood up and scanned their faces. Everyone looked bored. But as soon as Allen started sharing stories of healing, everyone's attention was riveted on him. For half an hour he told stories of God healing people, which gave him an opportunity to share the gospel.

As the time drew to a close, Allen said, "I have just a few minutes left. I was praying this morning and God showed me five health-related problems in this room that He's going to touch. I want you to take a risk and come up here, and I'm going to pray for you."

> As soon as Allen started sharing stories of healing, everyone's eyes were riveted on him.

Allen mentioned five conditions, including migraine headaches, chest pain, and knee problems. Five people came up to him. Allen took a deep breath and said to them, "This isn't up to me; it's up to the Holy Spirit. We're just going to invite Him to come, and we'll see what happens."

As he prayed, Allen invited the Holy Spirit to come, and He showed up! Allen saw the evidence in front of him. Some of the people started shaking; others became teary-eyed. The rest of the group sat there with their mouths wide open.

Allen talked to the people for whom he was praying. "What are you experiencing?" he asked each of them. "I feel hot all over," said one person. "I can feel energy going up and down my leg," said another.

After the meeting, other people made a beeline for Allen. One lady asked him for prayer right then. Another man asked Allen to meet him later to pray.

The following week at the business club meeting, people

thanked him and told him how impressed they were. One man, who came in late, interrupted the proceedings.

"I'm still trying to process last week's presentation," he said. "There are only three options. Number one, it was the power of positive thinking; number two, this was a serious case of mind control; or number three, we actually had an encounter with the God of the Bible. If you're planning on doing any more talks like this, count me in."

At the break, Allen stood up. "A number of you have expressed interest in what happened last week. My church runs a course called Alpha. It talks about developing a relationship with God. If anyone is interested, let me know."

Linda jumped to her feet. "I'll host it!" she said.

Five people came to the first meeting and began studying the Alpha course, a small-group discussion curriculum used worldwide, designed to help people discover the basics of Christianity in a nonthreatening environment. Each week, a key question is asked, such as, "Who is Jesus?" "How can we have faith?" and "What does the Holy Spirit do?" Several of the participants in Allen's group gave their lives to Jesus. One couple even destroyed thousands of dollars' worth of occult paraphernalia and books.

What to Do Next?

Two years prior to his involvement in the business club meetings, Allen was pastoring a legacy church. It had started when he received the notice from the church property's landlord that the rent was going to be doubled!

"There has to be a way to start churches that doesn't take so much money," Allen said to his wife, Kathie.

The church was hosting a speaker for a weekend conference on healing. In his final message, the speaker said that people should go out to preach the Kingdom and heal the sick. While the speaker was reading the Scriptures, Allen was struck not by the command to heal the sick, but by Jesus' words, "Go! I am sending you out!"

Jesus doesn't want His followers to have healing meetings and invite people to come. He is asking us to take the gift of healing to people in need. Allen was stunned by the thought.

When he arrived home, his brother Frank, who was also a pastor, was there. Allen's brother was in the process of starting a cell church in his city and had already started a couple of cell groups. But Frank was enjoying the small groups so much that he was reluctant to start a weekly celebration when all the groups came together.

Allen thought about transitioning his whole legacy church to a simple church model.

"That's it, Frank," exclaimed Allen. "I'll just keep multiplying small groups. That way we don't have to pay any rent."

Allen thought about transitioning his whole legacy church to a simple church model. But a house church leader he respected gave him different advice.

"Why in the world would you want to do that? Most people in your church didn't sign up for that. If you lead people down that path, it's going to kill you and it's going to kill the church. If you want to plant house churches, then you go do it!"

Allen met with the leadership team at his church and asked if they would release him to start house churches. "I feel like I'm a church planter at heart," he told them. "I loved my first four or five years here. But now I'm just in maintenance mode. I just have to do this."

A team assumed leadership of the church. Allen knew if he was going to ask people to start and lead house churches while they supported themselves with a job, he needed to set the example. He asked the church to cut his salary by two-thirds; he would supplement his income by returning to his former career in construction.

Two other couples joined Allen and Kathie as a church-planting team sent out by the legacy church. For the first couple of months, the group met together to pray and seek God. Because they were mostly families, they assumed they would grow by reaching other families. But when they started an Alpha course, mostly young singles attended. Allen's secretary at the construction company saw his heart for the lost. She invited her daughter, who brought some friends. The subsequent house group consists of the original three couples, plus the new believers from the Alpha course.

Allen retains a good relationship with the church he pastored. The two house churches—the one started by the team and the other that grew out of the business meeting—are considered outreaches of the church. Allen still preaches every couple of months and has been excited to see the legacy congregation's change of attitude about evangelistic outreach. A number of church members have started other Alpha groups in surrounding towns and have watched people coming to the Lord. The new believers are staying in their local groups and the people who lead the groups remain a part of the central church. Together they are seeing God's Kingdom grow.

Not only has Allen had an impact on his local church, but his national denominational leaders have given their blessing. They are open to exploring alternative ways of planting churches and have invited Allen to serve on a church-planting task force.

To Transition or Not to Transition?

Can a legacy church transition into a network of simple churches? There are some interesting points Jesus makes in the parable of new wine and new wineskins (Luke 5:37-39). First, Jesus was equally concerned for the new and the old wine—and consequently, the new and old wineskins. Jesus is as concerned about legacy churches and their members as He is about simple churches. So should we try to transition the whole church to the newer model? According to Jesus, if we do that, we may run the risk of ruining the old wineskin and spilling all the wine. We need to seek God for His will in our specific situation.

> *Jesus says that new wine needs to go into new wineskins.*

Jesus says that new wine needs to go into new wine-skins. When people become Christians, they usually will become stronger believers if they remain in a small group context within their own culture rather than come to "our" church—whether that is a legacy or simple church. It's even more effective when those believers open up their own sphere of influence for the Good News of the Kingdom. When that happens, the individual becomes a "person of peace" (see Rosa's story in chapter 6) and the focus of a new work of God.

When you read through the New Testament, you find groups of people becoming disciples together, rather than coming to faith as individuals (with a few notable exceptions such as Paul or the Ethiopian eunuch). Cornelius, Lydia, and the Philippian jailer were all baptized "with their households" (Acts 10:24, 48; 16:15, 33). When we bring people into our church culture, they quickly assimilate into that culture, often becoming isolated from their original friends and circle of influence and losing relevance to them. It is better to let them become "new wine in a new wineskin."

What happens when the leader of a legacy church catches a vision for a simpler model of church? Should he or she transition the whole church? Does a simple church or a network of simple churches need a pastor? Is his or her role now irrelevant? Usually a pastor and his family are dependent on the church for their livelihood. Unlike Allen, a pastor may not have the training or skills to change jobs. What will he or she do about finances?

There are now many churches around the country, from small community churches to megachurches, that have transitioned or are in the process of transitioning from a legacy church to a network of simple churches.[1] The Foursquare denomination has a simple church track[2] and many denominations are becoming increasingly open to these concepts. Other organizations are starting simple churches (see the students' stories in chapter 13); and many legacy churches, mission societies, and denominations that work in other countries are using the simple model of church in international situations.[3] Simple church leaders are working with other megachurches across the nation who want to encourage the simple, organic church movement.[4] When the Kingdom of God becomes our focus, churches of all kinds can work together.

What happens to the pastor of a legacy church if he or she transitions to a simple church? Sometimes the pastor finds a job. God seems to be giving many people creative business ideas. Sometimes the network of churches will continue to support the pastor until he or she finds some other means of producing income. Sometimes the pastor may raise support, as many missionaries do.

However, any church could do what Allen's church has done—encouraging people to start simple churches as an outreach from their legacy church. God will bless a church that gives away its best people to missions. He is debtor to no one. He will quickly replace both the people who leave and their finances! And the Kingdom of God will advance.

18

NO EMPIRE BUILDING, NO CONTROL, AND NO GLORY

The Man Who Loved to Help God's Kingdom Grow

Don't be selfish; don't try to impress others. Be humble, thinking of others as better than yourselves. Don't look out only for your own interests, but take an interest in others, too. You must have the same attitude that Christ Jesus had. Though he was God, he did not think of equality with God as something to cling to. Instead, he gave up his divine privileges; he took the humble position of a slave and was born as a human being. When he appeared in human form, he humbled himself in obedience to God and died a criminal's death on a cross. Therefore, God elevated him to the place of highest honor and gave him the name above all other names, that at the name of Jesus every knee should bow, in heaven and on earth and under the earth, and every tongue confess that Jesus Christ is Lord, to the glory of God the Father.

— PHILIPPIANS 2:3-11

✷ A true and safe leader is likely to be one who has no desire to lead,
but is forced into a position of leadership by the inward pressure of
the Holy Spirit and the press of the external situation. . . . A fairly
reliable rule of thumb [is] that the man who is ambitious to lead is
disqualified as a leader. The true leader will have no desire to lord
it over God's heritage, but will be humble, gentle, self-sacrificing,
and altogether as ready to follow as to lead, when the Spirit makes
it clear that a wiser and more gifted man than himself has appeared.
— A. W. TOZER, *The Reaper*

✷ Like the *Poseidon*, the kingdom of God is upside down; at least
it appears to be from our point of view. In God's kingdom, the
basement is the penthouse. The first become last, and the last are
first (Matt 19:30). The humble are exalted and the exalted are
humbled (1 Peter 5:5-6). . . . Are you seeing a pattern here? From
our worldly perspective, the kingdom of God is backwards. It is
upside down. In a sense, everything you think you know is wrong,
and everything you think is wrong is right. Wow! That is how
separate the kingdom of God is from this world.
— NEIL COLE, *Organic Leadership*

"Les, could we get together sometime? We're moving next month to be nearer our daughter and she's asked me to help her start a church in her home. I'm wondering if you have any ideas about how I could go about it."

"Sure, Jim! How about lunch together tomorrow?"

As Les hung up the phone, he thanked God for another opportunity to help someone start a simple church. He had known Jim for a number of years. Jim was fairly typical of the fastest-growing segment of Christians in the United States—believers who do not go to church.[1] Jim loved Jesus with all his heart but was floundering somewhat since leaving a traditional church. *Maybe this opportunity could give Jim some real direction in his walk with the Lord,* Les thought.

The restaurant was crowded, but Jim and Les found a corner table where they could talk undisturbed. Once the waitress had taken their order, they got down to business. Les flattened his paper napkin on the table and pulled out a pen.

First he drew two parallel lines of small boxes on his napkin. "These boxes represent the homes along a street." He put an X on one of the boxes. "Imagine that you lead someone in this house to the Lord—we'll call him Bob. If you invite Bob to the church you attend, he has to go down the road, across the railroad tracks, and way over to the other side of town where your church is located."

Les drew an arrow from the house with the X to the edge of the napkin. "Bob gets so busy in your church that he has no time left for the people on his street. Now imagine, instead of inviting Bob to your church across town, you start a church in his home. And one of the primary aims of that church is to reach Bob's family and neighbors."

Les drew some arrows from Bob's house to some of the other houses on the street.

"Then you have reached that community for the Lord," Jim said excitedly.

"Now suppose Bob's friend from work becomes a Christian. Should you bring him to Bob's home?"

"You could, but it would be more effective to start another church in his home!"

"You've got it! That way, you reach another community of people."

"Things could multiply very quickly if that really caught on!" The light was obviously going on in Jim's mind.

"Now let's go back to Bob's house," said Les. "Let's imagine that the church in Bob's house starts to grow, and it gets so big that there is no more room for people in Bob's living room. What would you do?"

"We could divide it into two," Jim suggested.

"That would be one possibility," Les agreed. "But there might be a better way."

He turned the napkin over and drew a circle. "Let's say this represents Bob's church. This is what you are suggesting."

Les drew two equal, smaller circles under the first one. "People who have split a home church in this way say that it feels like a divorce. Let's say Bob's home church is getting large enough to outgrow the living room, and some people are no longer participating as they did when it was smaller. Here's another option."

Les drew a small circle beside the original circle representing a home church, and an arrow going from the larger "church" to the smaller one.

"When a new person wants to join Bob's church, why not suggest that some people start a church at his house instead. That way, Bob's church has given birth to a daughter, rather than having a divorce. In fact, you don't have to wait until it's getting too big to birth a daughter church. If someone who seems like a 'person of peace'[2] joins Bob's church, you could start one with him anyway.

"All over the world, God is using rapidly multiplying simple churches to transform communities," explained Les. "The same could happen in this country too!

> **Simple churches reach people who wouldn't darken the doors of a church building.**

Simple churches are the obvious way to reach people who wouldn't darken the doors of a church building. But they will come into your home when invited.

"I've brought a book for you that I have found very helpful. It's published by House2House and it's called *Getting Started*.[3] It's a manual on how to start house churches. We've started more than a dozen churches by following the principles in it."

"Thanks, Les. I'll read it. It looks really interesting."

As their time together drew to a close, Les made a suggestion. "Let's keep in touch regularly on this. We could set up a monthly phone call so you can fill me in on how things are going. And if there's anything I can do to help, just let me know."

"I'd like that," said Jim. He thought for a moment. "Does this mean that any churches I start have to be a part of your network?"

"No, not at all," replied Les. "I'm not trying to build up Harvest Home Church Network. This isn't about building my empire or organization or expanding my sphere of influence. You and I are friends! This thing isn't organization based; it's relationship based. The apostle Paul was not an organizational figure in an early church hierarchy. Jesus is building His church. What's important is the Kingdom!

"Jim, I know this idea is contrary to all the church growth literature. This is your opportunity to expand the Kingdom and share Jesus. It's completely open and free. I believe the more I give it away, the more it will grow. You cannot out-give God!"

Jim followed Les's advice. Three months after moving, he had started three churches!

How It Began for Les

Les was a pastor in a traditional church for twenty-four years. During that time, the church had home groups, cell groups, zone meetings, and topical meetings. He always recognized the importance of the intimacy and relationship that occurs in a smaller group setting. But these small meetings were always feeder groups into "real" church on Sunday morning.

Les moved out of state to pastor a new church with cell

meetings. But people weren't being spiritually fulfilled because of its inward-looking nature. The motivation for the cells was still to build a typical Sunday morning church service, and over time Les could see that God's Kingdom wasn't expanding.

Les explains what happened next.

"I started meeting with other people in our area who are involved in house churches. I read *Houses That Change the World* by Wolfgang Simson and went to a house church conference, and my thinking began to change.

"Things clicked!" says Les. "Then I came across a book called *Simply Church*[4] and the *Getting Started* manual from House2House. The manual is helpful because it is practical. People read it and say, 'I can do that! I can open up my home and meet with people.'"

Initially, Les planned on starting three new churches. But one day when he was praying, he sensed the Lord speaking to him. "You are not to start three or four churches this year; that's your own thinking. You are going to start twelve!"

> "I can do that!
> I can open up my
> home and meet with
> people."

Les has done that and more. In fact, the network actually started around twenty churches and continues to expand with new churches emerging. A few of them have failed, but most are still going strong and people are becoming Christians. Some churches are local; some, like Jim's, are out of state. They have started churches in a low-income housing project and in different neighborhoods. Twenty-five committed

Christian students at a local university are in the process of starting three more groups. A tremendous ministry on high school campuses has taken off with an "adopt a school" approach, providing individual tutoring and mentoring in several high schools.

One group has reached out to the Muslim community; another group has started three messianic groups reaching the Jewish community. In addition, many individuals have been on short-term (three to six months) mission trips. One family is now serving full time in Mozambique and South Africa.

The leader of one of the churches in a subdivision feels strongly that he needs to pastor the people who live in his neighborhood, whether they know the Lord or not. If they need help, he wants to provide for them. For example, the church helped a single mother with three teenage kids find furniture, and then gave the family money at Christmastime.

One of the churches met in a local restaurant for over a year until it outgrew the small room they rented. A messianic group meets on Friday nights to celebrate the Jewish Sabbath and has another meeting in a local restaurant with more than twenty people studying Bible prophecy and current events every week.

Les's network of simple churches is called Harvest Home Church Network. But Harvest is part of a regional network of networks called Sojourners, which includes thirty to forty simple churches. The leaders meet regularly, and they all have the same heart to see their areas transformed.

Les has a pastor's heart. He loves to train leaders to pastor their groups effectively. He tells them, "Just keep in touch with people in a simple way. Find out how they are doing. Know what's going on in their lives.

"I can't say I'm not tempted, but I know that I'm not called to be a famous international speaker. I serve in the corner of the vineyard where God has placed me and I do what He's asking me to do. I don't see it as a springboard to fame and fortune."

No Empire Building, No Control, and No Glory

Les loves to give away what he is learning. He is not trying to expand his circle of influence or build his own little kingdom. God's Kingdom is far more important to him.

The Lord has given us a saying that characterizes this movement of simple, organic churches.

No empire building,

No control,

No glory!

At House2House, we frequently get calls from people asking us if they can join our network of House2House churches.

"I'm sorry, but there's nothing to join," we say. "We'll do everything we can to help you, but there is no House-2House network of churches."

Too often, people measure "success" in God's Kingdom by the world's standards. They are interested in numbers—of people, of dollars, of real estate. However, in the Kingdom, success is measured by intangibles—faithfulness, obedience to the Lord, character development (2 Peter 1:5-8). In other countries we have seen what happens when "apostles" grab for power by persuading churches to "come under their authority." The result is a tendency toward denominationalism, an unhealthy sense of competition, and lack of cooperation and unity across the body of Christ.

It would be easy for House2House to build its own empire, but we are determined not to do that. We don't even keep track of the number of churches across the country that start as a result of the resources we produce and conferences we run, for fear of being tempted to somehow claim credit for them. We don't trust ourselves with that kind of information.

Too often, people measure "success" in God's Kingdom by the world's standards.

The question of who is in control brings up similar concerns. Too many of our legacy churches are dominated by power struggles and control issues. *The people in the pew cannot be trusted to hear God for themselves,* those leaders seem to believe. *The only vision that counts is that of the senior pastor or the leadership team.* Whose church is this? It belongs to Jesus! He is the one building His church. He can be trusted to lead His people. And we can expect His people to hear Him.

In these simpler expressions of church, we long for Jesus to be the one in control. If someone hears the Holy

Spirit speaking to him or her giving a course of action, our response should be, "What can we do to support you? Do you need any resources? How can we help?" (see Ephesians 4:11-12).

The apostle Paul quite frequently left a church (often because he was thrown out of town) after just a few days or weeks (for example, Philippi in Acts 16:12 and Thessalonica in Acts 17:1-2). From that point on, he visited infrequently and communicated with them by letter. He was content to leave the church under the control of the Holy Spirit. We too need to trust the Holy Spirit.

A few years ago, John Arnott (from the Toronto Vineyard) wrote, "Seemingly, the Holy Spirit has no problem coordinating hundreds and thousands of different individuals and congregations for His eternal purposes. Things really do work much better when Jesus Himself is the head."[5]

No glory! How often have charismatic leaders within God's Kingdom been shipwrecked because they have taken God's glory for themselves? They are willing to let the fame and honor rub off on them. They delight in being praised and eagerly accept the applause and accolades of others.

Can any of us say that fame wouldn't affect us the same way? Only the Lord can keep our attitudes right; we cannot do it ourselves. Lord, don't let us touch Your glory!

Jesus can be trusted to lead His people. And we can expect His people to hear Him.

If we in simple churches think that we have a corner on the market of where God is really moving, we are deluding ourselves. God is at work in many different streams across the nation. As a movement, we need to make sure we stay humble, bow at the foot of the Cross, and willingly fellowship with any other believers, no matter which "stream" they belong to.

The history of various moves of God reveals that it doesn't take long before people start to take over—creating programs and plans that put God in a box and replacing the Holy Spirit with their own strategies and good ideas. Will this one be any different? Will we, as a movement, be able to resist the temptation to act as God?

"God, have mercy on us!"

19

THE BIGGER PICTURE

Watching God Move in a Powerful Way

Look around at the nations; look and be amazed! For I am doing something in your own day, something you wouldn't believe even if someone told you about it. — HABAKKUK 1:5

☼ Two out of three adults contend that they are not tied to a conventional church setting as they seek to experience and express their faith. This openness to new contexts, processes and structures is especially common among Baby Boomers (68%). . . . About 7% of adults attend a house church in a typical month, which is a seven-fold increase in the past decade.

— BARNA UPDATE, JUNE 2009

IN LATE 2000, two leaders from other networks of simple churches in central Texas approached us. Jim and David are good friends whom we have worked with for years. "We have a vision for a magazine for the house church movement," Jim shared with us. "Would you be willing to join us?"

We saw the value of a magazine when we were part of the British house church movement.[1] When we did some further research, it became apparent that many of the major moves of God over countless decades were somehow "represented" by a magazine[2]—the magazine often acting as a catalyst to further God's work.

We not only joined with Jim and David in their vision, we soon found ourselves carrying primary responsibility for the day-to-day operation of the magazine called *House2House*. Much to our delight and amazement, the magazine captured people's imaginations and was sent all over the world. It was a true periodical—we only produced the occasional printed copy when we had sufficient funds. With the changes in how people access information today as well as the need to be more cost-effective, the content now can be found on the Web site, http://www.house2house.com. Working with the magazine has been an incredible (and humbling) privilege for us, because people contact House2House to let us know what God is doing in their area. We receive e-mails or phone calls from people on a daily basis. The most frequent comment we get is:

"God led us to gather in our home, but we thought we were the only ones doing church that way. Then we came across the magazine [or Web site], and we discovered that God is doing this all over the country and across the world. We are part of a move of God's Spirit. We're not alone any longer!"

Some of our thinking about simple churches was originally influenced by a book that initially could only be downloaded from the Internet.[3] During our first visit to India, we met the book's author, Wolfgang Simson, and were impressed by the extent and clarity of his thinking about the nature of the church. (And we thought *we* were radical!)

"Would you be willing to come to the States and speak to us and some of our friends?" we asked him.

Wolfgang accepted our invitation for March 2001.

We sent out a few e-mails and invited people to a Saturday conference in our home. It wasn't long before we wondered if we had bitten off more than we could chew. We got the definite impression that more people were coming than we had anticipated.

Should we move the conference to a church building? We eventually decided to leave it in our home (after all, this was a conference on home church), borrowing extra chairs.

In the end, over a hundred sixty people came! (Fortunately, our current home has an open floor plan, and we actually managed to seat everyone. Our septic system did not cope quite as well, but that is another story!) Many of those who attended were challenged by what Wolfgang said. But perhaps the most important thing to come out of the day was the forging of friendships with others of like mind

across the country. Other connections have developed subsequently, and many of these deep friendships have proven
very strategic.

For several years, the network of churches we started
took a retreat together over Labor Day weekend. We initially used an old ranch house in the middle of nowhere
where we enjoyed the beautiful countryside and had a guest
speaker come to share from the Lord with us. As the numbers
increased, we graduated to a hotel in a nearby city. When
we opened the conference up to readers of the magazine, it
grew considerably. People from all over the country, and even
some from other nations, now attend the National House
Church Conference where various speakers share what they
sense God is saying to us.

The movement extends far beyond our involvement and
those with whom we work. According to research done by
George Barna, there are now between six million and twelve
million people in this country for whom their primary expression of church life is a simple church. What began as a fledg-
ling, ragtag group of nobodies has become a movement[4]—still
consisting of a nameless and faceless group of disciples meeting wherever life takes place and seeking to live a Kingdom
lifestyle.

That is perhaps one of the most exciting things about
what is going on. This movement is spontaneous. There is
no special location to visit, no superstar to follow. There
is no central organization. It appears that the Holy Spirit is
responsible for leading people all across the United States to

gather informally and reach out to their communities with the Good News of the Kingdom.

The current movement spans the whole spectrum of orthodox Christian theology—the distinctions are increasingly becoming blurred. For example, believers with a non-charismatic background are as likely to see a supernatural answer to prayer or have God clearly lead or speak to them as those embracing a charismatic theology. The stories in this book reflect that. Theology doesn't seem to divide us any longer.

With the emphasis less on church as a weekly event, living out the values and principles of the Kingdom has become more fluid and spontaneous, a clearer expression of family. Although we are aware of many simple churches that have been going on for decades, other simple churches seem to have a shorter life span. However, many exist longer than we had anticipated.[5] Often it seems that they are birthed, serve a purpose for a while, and rather than continue on indefinite life support without the presence of the Holy Spirit, are allowed to die. However, the relationships continue as new groups form.

> **Living out the principles of the Kingdom has become more fluid and spontaneous, a clearer expression of family.**

It has also been exciting to see the increasing collaboration across the body of Christ—simple churches working together with other expressions of the church for the sake of the Kingdom. It resonates with Jesus' longest recorded prayer in Scripture, where he prayed for unity in the body (John 17).

Some groups work at a national level to equip people. Greenhouse training takes place all over the United States (and in many other countries too), teaching people how to make disciples and start organic churches with people who do not yet know the Lord. The Lk10.com Web site is a community of practice for church planters. Simplechurch.com is a social networking site that carries various resources, including a six-week "Getting Started" course that equips people with some of the skills needed to work with a group of not-yet-believers. Blogs and Web sites such as House2House play an increasing role in the viral spread.[6]

It also has been a great privilege working with other like-minded visionaries from across the United States. We stay accountable to one another, seeking out opportunities to spend time with one another. There is no formal organization—it's just a group of friends listening to God together, duplicated over and over again by similar groups around the country.

A charismatic personality put on a pedestal is the last thing we want.

Several years ago, we discussed what to do when the concept of house or simple, organic churches reached a tipping point in the United States.[7] (A tipping point occurs when an idea becomes acceptable across a wide spectrum of society. We may already have reached that point.) I remember sitting in a meeting when a dozen or so of us came together to wait on the Lord for two days.

"How will we avoid the 'superstar mentality'?" someone asked. "When simple churches gain acceptance, people are bound to want to put a charismatic personality on a pedestal, and that's the last thing we want. Is there a way to prevent it?"

"It's not that the movement won't have leadership," added another. "But leadership has to be nonhierarchical—a humble servant seeking the good of others, not seeking the limelight."

"Maybe we should make sure that any media attention is shared among all of us," suggested one. "If, for example, someone is featured in a magazine article, and that leads to increased publicity, the next time the person is asked, he or she should say, 'Oh, I'm not the person you want to speak to! You should talk to so-and-so!'" Since that discussion, this actually has happened!

It is not just the Christian media that is paying attention. The secular media has shown interest too.[8] There have been articles in the press as well as television programs featuring what is going on in the simple church movement.

There are dangers in reaching the tipping point. We could become the latest fad, another church growth program that has gained in popularity, and people could merely jump on the bandwagon. For example, if churches start calling any small group a house or simple church, those groups face the danger of being an anemic counterfeit of the real thing. Equally, if charismatic leaders from within the movement itself try to seek prominence or decide to control what only God can do, or if we develop some kind of programmatic approach without being led by the Lord, we will destroy ourselves. Only God can keep us on track.[9]

It is becoming obvious that God is moving in this nation and across the Western world. We no longer have to go to Asia or Africa to see His hand at work. All over the country, God is leading His people to meet simply, in their homes or their places of work. The movement is very outward-focused, with an emphasis on reaching unbelievers.

House2House gives us a front seat in the arena of what God is doing with simple, organic churches across the Western world. The stories of what is happening are incredible! God is on the move!

A Church on the Move

For various reasons, church as we have always known it is becoming increasingly irrelevant in today's fast-paced society. Each week, thousands are leaving legacy churches, never to return.

In his thought-provoking book *The Present Future*, Reggie McNeal writes, "A growing number of people are leaving the institutional church for a new reason. They are not leaving because they have lost faith. They are leaving the church to preserve their faith."[10]

In fact, the fastest-growing segment of Christendom in the West today is that of Christians outside the legacy church. Many of them are mature, seasoned Christians,[11] no longer isolated and insulated from the rest of the world. They are an army, trained and available, who have caught the vision of multiplying simple churches and are reaching out to their communities.

Denominational leaders are becoming increasingly aware that the church in the United States is in a state of serious decline. Unless something changes, we are only one generation away from being a post-Christian society such as Europe, where Christianity has long since ceased being significant. These leaders can see that the vast majority of churches are not growing or even managing to keep up with the rate of U.S. population growth.

As these church leaders ask the Lord about this, many are concluding that the answer lies in simpler forms of church—just as in the rest of the world. Could they train and release their people to go out into their spheres of influence, make disciples, and start churches as part of their church's outreach efforts? This is already happening in legacy churches across the country.

The church in the United States is in a state of serious decline.

When the Bible was put into the hands of ordinary people back in the 1500s, the Reformation resulted. This did more than merely change the church; it transformed nations. In the same way that the man in the pew gained hold of the Bible during the Reformation, imagine what could happen if the church were released into the hands of ordinary people today.

There is an increasing hunger in this nation for an authentic spirituality. The signs are everywhere—in books, movies, and television. The fields are ripe and ready to harvest. The majority of workers for the harvest may come from that harvest. As new people within this movement of God become disciples, a part of their DNA will begin to multiply. They are probably the best resource for the harvest.

This nation will be transformed only as an army of ordinary people are willing to get out of their comfortable pews or armchairs to tell the world the Good News: Jesus still heals the sick and sets the captives free. When ordinary Christians say yes to God and move out into their neighborhoods or their workplaces to make disciples and start simple churches among those who are not yet Christians, we will see a spectacular advance in the Kingdom.

This army of ordinary believers is already mobilizing. The Western world is about to see what happens when the ordinary believer goes into action for the Kingdom.

You, too, could have a story like the ones in this book. Are you ready to enlist?

Do you have a story? We invite you to share it with us at http://www.TonyandFelicityDale.com.

20

PARADIGM SHIFTS

How Our Perspectives Have Changed

Over the past fifteen years, as Tony and I have traveled along this path of the simple, organic, or house church, certain concepts have totally altered the way we live or think about and practice church—once we have truly grasped them.

Here are the main ones:

1. *Church genuinely is "where two or three are gathered together in His name."* This understanding of church turned our lives upside down. When we realized that church was neither buildings nor an event (namely meetings), but relationship with Jesus and with His people, it became a 24/7 Kingdom lifestyle. It meant that church could be as simple as gathering together with a group of friends over a meal to share Jesus together. We are not church just because we are in a special building at a special time with special people leading us. We are church when we are together in His name. Not only that, almost anyone can start a church if it is just a few friends coming together!

2. *Jesus is to be the head of His church.* The key skill in simple church life is listening to the Lord and then responding to what He says—whether that is in our lives as individuals or in the body of Christ together as we hear Him through each other. Our obedience will result in both community and mission.

3. *God's heart is for the harvest.* Church is meant to be missional rather than attractional. Jesus said to His disciples, "Go" (Mark 16:15) and, "As the Father has sent me, so I am sending you" (John 20:21). The passage in Luke 10 provides principles that help us out of our Christian enclaves into a world that is seeking spiritual truth.

4. *Churches are meant to multiply.* Every living thing God has created reproduces after its kind. Churches are not meant to be sterile. We give birth to new churches by working with groups of not-yet-believers out in the harvest and seeing them become disciples together.

5. *The resources are in the harvest.* The "person of peace" principle means that workers for a particular segment of society are to be found within that people group or subculture. It is more effective for the Kingdom to begin in the home of the person of peace and with the people that he or she knows than to invite that person to come to our church.

If the resources are in the harvest, it means that our next generation of leaders may not even be Christians yet. We love watching a person become a Christian, introduce his friends to Jesus, and end up leading a church under the mentorship of a more mature believer.

6. *Simple is reproducible; complex is not.* Most churches are all about raising the bar, creating a higher standard, whether that is in leadership, teaching, or worship. Simple church is about lowering the bar, making it possible for everyone to get involved.

7. *Keep it small.* There are more than fifty commands in the New Testament that include the words "one another." These commands only make real sense within a small-group context. We need to multiply the small, not look to grow ever larger. If we are getting to a size where these commands cannot be obeyed, it's time to multiply!

> **Simple church makes it possible for everyone to get involved.**

8. *Practice the priesthood of all believers.* We are a Kingdom of priests (1 Peter 2:9). All the members of the body of Christ are important. Each of us has direct connection to our Head, Jesus. We no longer need an intermediary to go to the throne room for us. It's time for the clergy/laity distinction to end. Jesus used ordinary, untrained people to change the world.

This is not a mere theological truth. It needs to become a practical reality in our lives together. When we get together, each of us is meant to take part. Each one of us has a contribution to make to our shared lives (1 Corinthians 14:26).

9. *Christianity needs to be nonreligious.* Jesus Himself was not religious, and Christianity is not meant to be a rule book or a series of laws that we are punished for if we break them. When we become Christians, God gives us new hearts of flesh with His laws written on them. If we live spontaneously

from our hearts, we will find ourselves living a life that is pleasing to Him. We no longer have to color inside the lines. God is not sitting up in heaven with a big stick waiting to catch us in some sin. A life lived from the heart is very attractive to unbelievers.

10. *Leadership is servanthood.* Jesus meant it when He said leadership within His Kingdom is not like leadership in the world. He gave us a practical example of how it should look when He washed His disciples' feet. Jesus literally laid down His life for others. As we die to ourselves and any desire for control or the limelight, our lives will reflect His attitude of servanthood.

21
WHERE DO YOU GO FROM HERE?

IF THE CONCEPTS presented through these stories grabbed your attention, and if you are sensing the Lord may want you to take these ideas further, here are some suggested resources for you as you seek the Lord.

Recommended Reading

The Rabbit and the Elephant by Tony and Felicity Dale and George Barna

The House Church Book by Wolfgang Simson

Simply Church by Tony and Felicity Dale

Getting Started by Felicity Dale

Revolution by George Barna

Pagan Christianity? by Frank Viola and George Barna

Reimagining Church by Frank Viola

The Global House Church Movement by Rad Zdero

Nexus edited by Rad Zdero

Church Planting Movements by David Garrison

Organic Church by Neil Cole

Organic Leadership by Neil Cole

Church 3.0 by Neil Cole

ReJesus by Michael Frost and Alan Hirsch

Megashift by James Rutz

Web Sites

House2House, http://www.house2house.com

Luke 10: A Community of Practice, http://www.lk10 .com

Church Multiplication Associates, http://www .cmaresources.org

A social networking site for those involved in simple church, http://www.simplechurch.com

Videos

Tidal Wave, available for free download on http://www .simplechurch.com or http://www.house2house.com

When You Come Together, available for free download on http://www.simplechurch.com or http://www .house2house.com

Church Planting Movements, available from the International Mission Board of the Southern Baptist Convention at http://www.imb.org

Further Training

A Getting Started course can be accessed at http://www.simplechurch.com

Greenhouse at http://www.cmaresources.org

Blogs

http://guymuse.blogspot.com

http://www.simplychurch.com

http://cole-slaw.blogspot.com

http://www.simplechurchjournal.com

http://www.davidlwatson.org

http://leavethebuildingblog.com

Acknowledgments

MY HEARTFELT THANKS go to all those who were willing to risk telling their stories for this book. Without their collaboration this book would not have been possible. My thanks also to the many family members and friends who read it story by story and then gave their advice and encouragement, and to the wonderful editorial team at Tyndale House Publishers who took my finished product and improved it beyond recognition.

Lastly, my thanks go to my husband, Tony, whose unfailing love and support are beyond price.

Notes

Chapter 1: God Uses Ordinary People to Do the Extraordinary

1. *Legacy church* is a term we use for a more traditional form of church because we so value the spiritual legacy we have received from them.

2. Henry T. Blackaby, *Experiencing God* (Nashville: B&H Publishing Group, 2007), 101–117.

3. When the Communists took over China in 1949, there were estimated to be one million Christians in that nation. Since that time, despite intense persecution resulting in many of the leaders being killed or thrown in prison, the church has grown exponentially. Our good friend Curtis Sergeant has extensive knowledge of the work in China. In an e-mail message to Felicity Dale on July 22, 2008, he wrote:

> Mr. Ye Xiaowen, the director of China's State Administration of Religious Affairs (the highest Communist Party official in charge of all religious affairs), in two meetings at Beijing University and in the China Academy of Social Sciences, claimed the number of Christians in China, including both the underground and the government-sanctioned churches, both Catholic and Protestant, has

reached 130 million members. A lot of people now cite those figures. There is a reasonable chance that there is some overlap among those groups. I personally use a number of 100 million, seeking to compensate for some of the overlap and to take out a percentage of [those who] may not be born again.

4. Tony and I recently had a phone conversation with a friend of ours who has a network of house churches in central and northern India. He encouraged his network to baptize all their new believers on the same day as a gift to God, commemorating the birthday of the church. On the Day of Pentecost 2009, they baptized more than 250,000 people.

Chapter 2: What Is Church?

1. Mark 4:14
2. C. Peter Wagner, *Church Planting for a Greater Harvest* (Ventura, CA: Regal, 1990), 7–8.
3. In charismatic circles, this is referred to as a "word of knowledge." A word of knowledge occurs when God supernaturally gives a piece of information to a person that no one would naturally know.
4. Galatians 6:2
5. Colossians 3:16
6. Rolland and Heidi Baker have written an account of this in their book *Always Enough* (Grand Rapids, MI: Chosen Books, 2003).
7. See the home page for Iris Ministries, Inc. at http://www.irismin.com.
8. Since that time, the Indian government has done an amazing job of rehousing the homeless in the cities. The slums have been razed and the people now live in government housing. On our last visit to Chennai in 2008, there were virtually no people sleeping on the streets. However, the villages remain as poor as ever.
9. On a 2009 trip to India, we met two middle-aged housewives who have trained other women to start churches.

This army of ordinary housewives has started a combined total of 8,000 churches.

10. Matthew 11:19

Chapter 3: The 10:2b Virus

1. This is a term and concept coined by church planter Wolfgang Simson.

2. One expression of this can be found at http://www .coloradohousechurch.com.

3. "Breakfast with David Yonggi Cho and Rick Warren," Pastors.com, 2001, http://legacy.pastors.com/rwmt/article .asp?ArtID=578.

4. David Watson, "Church Planting Essentials—Prayer," TouchPoint: David Watson's Blog, December 27, 2007, http://www.davidwa.org/node/27.

Chapter 4: The Great Commission

1. David Kinnaman, *unChristian* (Grand Rapids, MI: Baker Books, 2007), 27.

2. Neil Cole, *Organic Church* (San Francisco: Jossey-Bass, 2005).

Chapter 5: Bearing Much Fruit

1. John 12:24, NASB

2. The concepts of *attractional* and *liquid church* are discussed more fully in two books: Michael Frost and Alan Hirsch, *The Shaping of Things to Come* (Peabody, MA: Hendrickson Publishers, 2003) and Pete Ward, *Liquid Church* (Peabody, MA: Hendrickson Publishers, 2002).

Chapter 6: Luke 10 Principles

1. In charismatic circles, this would be known as the gift of prophecy or word of knowledge.

Chapter 7: The Holy Spirit Leads Us

1. Wolfgang Simson has been involved in extensive global research on growing churches, church-planting movements,

revival, and mission breakthroughs. He has written several books including *The House Church Book* and *The Starfish Manifesto* (the latter is only available online).

Chapter 9: Jesus Is Building His Church
1. See Robert Fitts's Web site at http://www.robertfitts.com.
2. A. W. Tozer, *The Quotable Tozer*, vol. 2 (Camp Hill, PA: Christian Publications, 1994), 78.
3. See http://www.keepingfaithsimple.com.

Chapter 10: Church Is Built on Relationships
1. In C. S. Lewis's Chronicles of Narnia series, Aslan the lion is an allegory for Jesus.

Chapter 11: Church Is Family
1. A more direct word from God, such as Joy and Stephen sometimes experienced, is known by some people as prophecy. Prophecy, revelation, and words of knowledge are usually referred to as "gifts of the Spirit." They are detailed in 1 Corinthians 12 and are ways that God may speak to people. For example, prophecy is a person speaking words that he hears God speaking into his heart or mind. The scriptural guidelines for prophecy are found in 1 Corinthians 14:3—prophecy is to be used for edification (building up), exhortation (encouragement), and comfort. The Scriptures instruct us to weigh prophecy; i.e., not merely to let it pass over our heads, but to assess whether it is from God and how to apply it to our lives. Words of knowledge occur when God supernaturally gives information about a person's life, and they are often used to cause faith to rise up in that person.
2. A recent survey conducted by Steve Lyzenga of House2Harvest.com for his doctoral dissertation has shown that simple churches are actually longer lived than we had originally thought. His results show that the churches surveyed had been in existence for an average of 5.06 years. If the ones that had been in existence for more than twenty years were removed, the average age was 3.75 years.

3. Neil Cole has written an excellent book called *Organic Leadership* that examines this subject. These ideas are also expanded in chapter 17 of *The Rabbit and the Elephant*, a book that Tony and I wrote with George Barna.

Chapter 13: Service and Strategy
1. "Obedience based" implies that any principle taught is put into practice as part of the course.
2. Mission Arlington serves the community with many different practical ministries that include health care, food, job assistance, a Christmas store, and much more. See http://www.missionarlington.org.
3. David Garrison's book *Church Planting Movements* provides more details about what the International Mission Board of the Southern Baptist Convention is seeing happen.

Chapter 14: Stone Soup Church
1. Academic Skills Center, "Active Study," Dartmouth College, http://www.dartmouth.edu/~acskills/docs/study_actively.doc.

Chapter 15: Discipleship and Training
1. Ninety-seven leaders representing fifty-three organic churches contributed to the 2007 "House Church Report" which was conducted by Ed Stetzer's ministry on behalf of Leadership Network. The results indicated that 82 percent of the leaders were being mentored and/or coached by other individuals as one of their primary means of training, which is important in a multiplication movement. Significantly, discipleship in organic churches was occurring in 79 percent of those in the survey group. The fifty-three organic churches represented in the survey started fifty-two new churches in 2006 alone—almost a 100 percent rate of reproduction. Over the past five years 30 percent of their daughter churches have started granddaughter churches. That is a high level of missional fertility within a Western context. CMA is also seeing a high percentage of conversion growth among their churches in the United States, with slightly more than 25 percent of

their growth through people coming to Christ for the first time. This would not be a high rate in China or India, but in a country where around 75 percent of people consider themselves already "Christian," this is a significant rate of conversion. A quarter of those coming into the movement are turning from darkness into the light.
2. "Discipling Viral Disciplers," May 6, 2009, http://www .simplechurchjournal.com/2009/05/discipling-viral-disciplers .html.
3. Kent Smith, "The Dawn Texas Project: A Harvest Force Report" (private research project, 2003–2004).

Chapter 16: Kingdom Finances and Kingdom Kids
1. See Acts 4:34-35; 11:28-30; and 2 Corinthians 8:1-5.
2. 1 Thessalonians 2:9
3. Acts 20:34
4. For example, 1 Corinthians 16:19.
5. George Barna, *Revolution* (Carol Stream, IL: Tyndale House Publishers, 2006), 33.
6. This was part of Steve Lyzenga's dissertation, "Assessing the State of Simple Churches in the USA Regarding Releasing Resources toward Finishing the Great Commission," for his doctor of ministry degree from Regents University, completed in May 2009.
7. John L. Ronsvalle and Sylvia Ronsvalle, *The State of Church Giving through 2000* (Empty Tomb, 2002), 13.

Chapter 17: To Transition or Not to Transition?
1. Some examples can be found at http://bridgepoint.org; http://www.apexcommunity.org; http://www.leavethebuilding .com; and http://www.vineyardcentral.com.
2. See http://reachmore.foursquare.org.
3. NorthWood Church in Keller, Texas, is a good example. The International Mission Board of the Southern Baptist Convention has also pioneered in these areas. Their video *Like a Mighty Wave* can be downloaded from http://www .imb.org.

4. Examples include the Austin Stone Community Church at http://www.austinstone.org and Northland, A Church Distributed at http://www.northlandchurch.net.

Chapter 18: No Empire Building, No Control, and No Glory

1. See *Revolution* by George Barna or visit http://barna.org/barna-update/article/5-barna-update/169-rapid-increase-in-alternative-forms-of-the-church-are-changing-the-religious-landscape.
2. See Rosa's story in chapter 6 for a description of a "person of peace."
3. Felicity Dale, *Getting Started: A Practical Guide to Church Planting* (Austin, TX: Karis Publishing, 2003). The principles in this book can also be found in a six-week training course under the "Getting Started" tab on www.simplechurch.com.
4. Tony and Felicity Dale, *Simply Church* (Austin, TX: Karis Publishing, 2002).
5. John Arnott, "Let's Get Back to Supernatural Church!" *Spread the Fire*, no. 5 (2004), http://www.tacf.org/Portals/18/docs/stf/stf%2010-5.pdf.

Chapter 19: The Bigger Picture

1. *Restoration* and *Fullness* were both magazines that served the British house church movement.
2. An example would be *Leaves of Healing* in the healing ministry of Scottish evangelist John Alexander Dowie in the late nineteenth century.
3. The book was *Houses That Change the World* by German house church planter Wolfgang Simson. It has been republished by Tyndale House Publishers as *The House Church Book*.
4. We now feel free to call this a movement because of the numbers involved. A group of strategists with whom I am in regular contact has come up with the following characteristics of a movement:

- It generates momentum, attracting and uniting people with like passions.
- People start doing similar things because of shared values.
- Usually there is a quick change in a relatively short amount of time—the concept of the tipping point.
- There is a change in public perception.
- There are people who are change agents/catalysts (often a group of people at the grassroots level).
- There is a climate for change that either exists or is set by the catalysts.
- An appetite and energy for change often begins with younger people.
- A movement is often a reaction to the status quo—hence persecution may follow.

There are three structural components to a movement (according to studies in 1970 by Luther Gerlach and Virginia Hine):

Decentralization: Things don't just happen with one leader or in one place
Segmentation: Things may look different in different places but they share similar values
Interconnection: Those involved in the movement are able to connect together
(Information in this note compiled from my blog at www.simplychurch.com.)

5. Steve Lyzenga of House2Harvest discovered some interesting facts in the survey for his doctoral dissertation. He writes, "The average age is 5.06 years with a range from 6 months to 40 years. If I remove the one at 40, the average drops to 4.78. If I remove three more at 30, the average drops to 4.15. If I remove three more at 20, the average drops to 3.75." Remember, these are churches that are still in existence!

6. Great blogs on simple church include SimpleChurch Journal at http://www.simplechurchjournal.com; The M Blog at http://guymuse.blogspot.com; and TouchPoint at http://www.davidlwatson.org.

7. This concept comes from Malcolm Gladwell's book, *The Tipping Point* (New York: Back Bay Books, 2002).

8. For example, articles such as "Going to Church by Staying at Home: Clergy-Less Living Room Services Seen as a Growing Trend" in the *Washington Post*, http://www.washingtonpost.com/wp-dyn/content/article/2006/06/03/AR2006060300225.html, and "There's No Pulpit Like Home," in *Time*, http://www.ptmin.org/TIME.pdf.

9. For a more complete treatise of this subject, see *The Rabbit and the Elephant* by Tony and Felicity Dale and George Barna (Carol Stream, IL: Tyndale House Publishers, 2009), chapters 20 and 21.

10. Reggie McNeal, *The Present Future* (San Francisco: Jossey-Bass, 2003), 4.

11. See http://www.openheaven.com/forums/printer_friendly_posts.asp?TID=4477.

Tony & Felicity Dale

Tony and Felicity Dale would love to keep in touch with you and let you know about other resources that they have produced. These resources include a regular e-letter that goes out to people around the world, as well as DVDs that help to explain more fully what simple church movements look like in practice.

For more information, please visit
www.tonyandfelicitydale.com.

Barna Books encourage and resource committed believers seeking lives of vibrant faith—and call the church to a new understanding of what it means to be the Church.

For more information, visit www.tyndale.com/barnabooks.

BARNA

CP0309

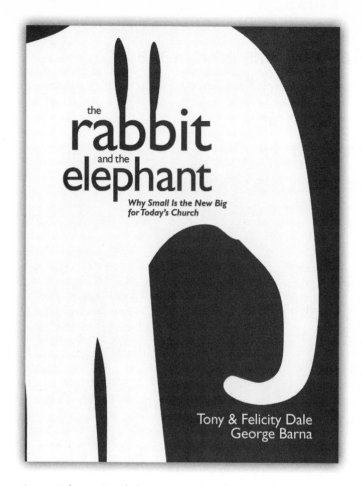

the
rabbit
and the
elephant

Why Small Is the New Big for Today's Church

Tony & Felicity Dale
George Barna

In ***The Rabbit and the Elephant,*** church planters Tony and Felicity Dale and acclaimed researcher George Barna use a simple analogy to bring a big message to God's church. How could we change the world if our Christian faith began multiplying at a rapid pace—through a way of life that is explosive and transformational?

978-1-4143-2553-8 (hardcover)

CP0394